Poetic Justice & Theory

A world of possibilities not yet imagined.

Written by Patience Zero

Because the world is not ready to comprehend:

<u>The Sit Down</u>

CONTENTS

"Coloring the Blind"

The color green is the sour taste of a lime with the crisp texture of lettuce and other leafy treats. The color green is a tree of butterflies fluttering in the wind, latched to the living wood's limbs. The color green is the envy inside the eyes of all who resent one another for various reasons of their own mind's perception. The color green is beautiful and bright but can also be dark and ugly. The color green paints the ocean forests of the world with its ugly beautiful blanket of bright darkness. The beautiful blanket of ocean forest is quilted together with patches of burnt or chopped plots of naked earth. The naked earth births new colors of green with time, patience, water, and sun. The new green would have never been birthed without the destruction of the earth's previous greenery. The color green smells like pine and mint. The smell of green is sour and tart but delicious and sweet. The color green reeks of a wretched jealousy stench. The color green is the feeling on your feet's flesh when you step onto a newly showered lawn. The feeling of green is a cool minty breeze as you walk through the forest. The color green is a professional pubescent with a large spectrum of personalities and moods. The color green identifies as no gender and is perfectly themself with their individual shades of freedom. The color green is the currency we use in monetary transactions. The color green is abundance and prosperity cursed by a wicked witch of antipathy and loathing. Green is everywhere in everything. The color green is alive in us all.

The color blue is water, it is fluid throughout the world's globe. The world itself is blue from an extraterrestrial point of view. The color blue is our sky on most days of the year. The color blue is the feeling of sadness and disappointment. The color blue is the ocean of our physical realm producing oddities and spectacles of nightmarish delight. The world of liquid delight is home to nightmares that live and feed in the depths of blue. The color blue is transphobic and identifies as a male, or a baby boy during a reveal party. The color blue is beautiful and can be chosen at will for any gender, or whatever, to paint as they wish their physical necessities of nature. The color blue is the bruise on your body that still hurts as it heals. The blue hue can be bright but sad. Blue shades vary from morbidly dark dwellings of the mind to a bright and pleasant, beautiful sky. The shades of blue are on a spectrum of mood and murkiness. The color blue is an oceanic splash of moist droplets that mist your face or body. The beautiful blue hue can absorb rays of attention, or the melancholy color can also hide in plain sight as a neutral color of bland blue bystander. The significance of blue is interpreted as it is advertised by its masters. The generic color blue is unlike other colors and can be uniquely identified as blue in the appropriate shade. The color blue is made from emotion. The color blue is the offspring of primary thoughts who mate as they wish for the world's colorful order. The color blue is alive in us all.

The color red smells like roses and flows entirely through your perfect bag of bones. The color red is the color of love, and arrogantly shames other colors for attempting to credit themselves with loving attributes. The bloody color is beautiful. The color red tastes like watermelon and cherries with notes of negativity. The color of red is a blanket of hugs and kisses warm to the touch and firm with distinction. The red color is a stopping signifier with written words crossed in red's powerful ink. The red smell of color is hatred, conservatorship, and communism all sleeping together on a bed of peppermints and thorny flowers. The color red is your eye's veins surrounding your pupils and irises becoming more vibrant with fatigue and flavorful substance. The color red is your flushed face in a moment of embarrassment. The red flushed embarrassment can transition to a red rage quickly triggered by a colorful catalyst. The color red splatters the walls of rage and violence. Seeing red is not a painting of physical sight, but a temporary tantrum of rage and momentary mania. The red color succubus is sexual and teases those who adorn her. The bloody red color is radically royal and sits on a throne of primary selection. The color red bleeds with promiscuous whispers of luscious love notes wrapped with lacey love lingerie. The taste of red is metallic like blood but can also be fruity or spicy. The spicy red shades taste like pepper-spray mouth mace and spark fires on your tongue's palate. Red is a lovely blood color that flaunts her sexual spice by flowing in all creatures of life. The color red is alive in us all.

The color yellow is the warm blanket of sunshine on a summer's day accompanied by an ice-cold glass of lemonade. The lemony yellow color is bright and has a small scale of light to dark; the darker the yellow, the more it fades to brown which is not yellow. Yellow is unique and signifies slow speeds of caution. Yellow is primary in the world's colorful scheme of wonder. Standing alone yellow is unmatched with its corny hue, but when mixed with other colors it births an infinite spectrum of shades that paint our physical realm with an array of diversity. Yellow is loud and speaks volumes about its primary position in the colorful world's order. Yellow tastes like bananas and buttery popcorn, but not together. The buttery yellow color melts with clarity as its own unique beam of light. The color yellow is cautious and clear. The color yellow is constructive and paints large machinery that perform tasks too great for man. The color yellow can be cheesy and shredded upon request. The yellow color is the sun itself and the power of our infinite grid of electricity. The electric color can be cowardice and shameful. The color yellow sounds like the chirps of a hundred baby chicks waiting to be adorned by anyone who see their cute chirping bodies. The sound of yellow is also a warning alarm indicating potential danger to anyone who hears her voice. The color yellow is sand between your toes and sun on your face. The color yellow is a cheesy sun banana that melts from its own buttery taste. The color yellow is alive in us all.

The color purple is an explosion of creativity and can only be seen when other colors congregate. The color purple is an exotic flower with unique pedals and tasty fruits. The purple of my mind is jams and jellies being slathered onto a toasted slice of bread. The color purple is cheerful and tastes like plums, grapes, and berry pies. The color purple is messy and carefree. The color purple is a talking caterpillar smoking a hookah. The purple color sits on a smaller scale of shades that is pinched between pink to the bright side, and black to the dark. The

3

dark side of purple is equally beautiful as its brighter counterpart. The purple smell of berries and exotic fruit is appetizing and waters your mouth with aromathera-berry. The color purple pops with peculiar promiscuity. The color purple grew up as a feminine identifier; however, in the current world of 21st century, the color is free and roams the earth with fluent language of cosmic abundance. The purple cosmic color is star dust and reaches the outer edges of our universe clouding galaxies billions of light-years away. The color purple is beautiful, like the rest of its siblings. Purple is proud to be purple, pinched in a small spectrum, spanning the universe's expansive reach. The color purple is an alien that sails the seas of space as dust and particulate powder. The color purple accompanies blue on your bruised skin waiting to heal. The purple hue is commonly mistaken and takes credit for red's loving attributes, but the color red is arrogant and shames purple for pridefully masking its mysterious face. The color purple is alive in us all.

The color orange tastes like fruity citrus seduction and smells of sour sweetness. The color orange feels like a fall day in October while walking through a pumpkin patch. The color orange is a round fruit that falls from trees filled with green butterflies. The orange color is candy for the eyes, ears, and mouth. The orange color sounds like Halloween music and sends a chill down your spine. The color orange is a safety spectacle of yellow and red's offspring; however, the parents cannot take credit for orange's beautiful features of variety. The orange color is not a color at all, but a flavor of sight seasoned with pumpkins, fruits, and fire. The fiery orange color is hot and glows with burning behavior of flaming flamboyancy. The color orange's embers burn themselves into dark coals as the bright orange hue fades to a dark brown on the color's scale. Orange is loud and gossips to red and yellow about its unique qualities that it stole from its gossiping group. The orange color is festive and explodes with purple in firework displays of celebration. Just like purple, orange is an alien. Orange is extraterrestrial and orbits the earth as less of a UFO, but more of an identifiable oddity of flight. The color flies without wings and is universal to the world's colorful palate. Orange is defined by its

4

own name, yet it would not exist without its parents, red and yellow. The color orange is arrogant, like red, but sits on its own extraterrestrial throne of uniqueness. The color orange is tasty, arrogant, sour, beautiful and loud. The color orange is alive in us all.

The color black is darkness for eternity. Black is beautiful, and bright with darkness. Black need not descriptions in words to explain her attractiveness, one must only shut their eyelids to observe the vast vanity of black's beauty. Black is nighttime fatigue, or an abrupt wakening in the dark hours of the morning. Black is mysterious and wonderful. The color black is universally unique and absorbs the other colors into its limitless abyss of dark cosmic space. The color black is the opposite of white, but only in humble hues, not in political patriotism. Blackness is the cosmos itself and is a vacuum of infinity. The color black is the universe's favorite color as it absorbs the other colors and paints the majority of our spacious existence. Speckled into black's infinite abyss of cosmos are galaxies of exploding spirals painted in a variety of colors. The color black is lonely and holds the other colors in her hands watching as they paint the universe with diversity. Black's hands hold the rainbow of our realm, and she observes as each color explodes itself from her handheld launchpad into the infinite abyss of space and time. Like black's opposite, white, black is blindness. To live in the complete darkness of black is a mental misinterpretation rather than a physical disability. Black can be shiny, dull, or dirty. The color black absorbs everything and is the dead-end finish line to any and all existence. Black is not only the ending but also the beginning. As a black hole is defined, the color black itself has a gravitational field that forbids any radiation of color to escape its abyss. Black is the bed of darkness cradling our colorful galaxies. The color black has no unique smell, taste, or sound, but is the compilation of all universal colors that she holds in her unique hands. The color black is alive in us all.

The color brown is a puddle of mud and the woody stump that holds green butterflies. Brown is not difficult to create and is experienced when multiple colors launch into each other from black's cosmic hands. The brown shades are natural and abundant in the world's colorful palate. The color is earth's land-body and produces varieties of green, among an abundance of other colors, when mixed with patience, liquid blue, and warm yellow sunlight. Brown is what most other colors fade too as they scale to the dark side. Brown is neutral yet comprised of other colors from the black infinite universe. Brown absorbs most colors and only evolves into a different shade of its own descent. The color brown sits on a humungous scale from light to dark with the word, tan, being a common choice to describe its individuality. The brown tan is also your sun burnt skin after it has healed from its red burn and faded to a darker version of your original tone. Brown is your healthy bowel movements consisting of all the previously eaten colors but also your beautiful log cabin surrounded by brown wood stumps holding green leafy butterflies. Brown is your caffeinated coffee at whatever time you desire. The color brown has many tastes but the sweetest of which is chocolate fudge. The color brown can smell like chocolate but can also smell disgusting like burnt hair or worse. The color brown is your unfinished wooden furniture that still produces sharp splinters. The color is dead green butterflies that fell from its wooden mother. The fallen dead brown color absorbs itself back into the earth's land-body. The color brown is a cycle of colorful life. The color brown is alive in us all.

The color white is bright and blinding. The color white is a snowy wonderland on a cold winter's day. White is the opposite of black, and it repels the other colors, it does not absorb. The color white is ice and freezing temperatures. Since the color white reflects other colors, the color white can often be deceptive and mirrors its neighboring color with its own reflection. The color white can be splattered with other colors creating a colorful mosaic of innovative explosions. White is beautiful, like all colors, as it reflects anyone who stands next to her. She kisses her neighbor with soft chilly lips of snow as the kissy neighbor is complimented with icy bling. White is the paper we ink colorful notes upon. The color white can be salty but sweet, reflecting whoever stands in its mirror. The color white is a dollop of sour cream on your brown baked potato, or a dollop of whipped cream on your flavorful, yellow-split sundae with a round red on top. The color white tastes like vanilla. The color white is versatile, like all other colors. White can be considered clean, fresh, and new; however, so can all the other colors. A fresh set of pearly whites guards your own mouth, chewing whatever color may enter its gates. The color white is the soft tissue paper you use to wipe colorful substances from various body parts. White surrounds your eyeball's irises and pupils, gradually threatened by red's veiny fatigue and flavorful substance. The color white, as all colors, is just a color, a measurement of sight, creativity, and uniqueness. Of all colors, there is none superior to another, and all have attributes of greatness. In a world full of colorful beings, I wish to be colorblind but explode with colorful collaborations; however, I am not colorblind. I see colors in all of their beauty, uniqueness, darkness, and deliverance. The colors of the world are alive in us all.

"Clouds"

I woke up on number nine. It was surreal and unlike numbers one through eight. Number nine is like an imaginative never-ending Rollercoaster of different stories compiled into a novel. The number nine novel is silver-lined and sharp with quick quips of character and charisma. Number nine is stitched with cuddly and loving pillows of pleasure. I woke up with energy and an electric feeling of power on number nine. I wish to live infinitely on number nine and its cuddly pillows of pleasure. I fear any more numbers may deplete my soul completely of the love and care that was drained from numbers four through eight. I wish for my love and care to fill the insides of number nine's pleasure pillows eternally comforting whoever wakes up on number nine beside me.

Numbers eight, seven, and six, were horrific. It was like hell but worse. The scorching heat from the hell fire that is six, seven and eight has burned my body completely and I remain blistered from their fiery facade. The three long numbers were excruciating and will forever be bound in the novel of number nine. The six, seven, and eight were incredibly dreadful with lessons of loathing lectures given by farce familiar peers. The peers were not peers at all, but nightmares who got lost on six, seven, and eight's hellish steps. The steps of hell begin at six and end just before the ninth gate.

Number five was boring and bland. It was less than hell but equal to an uncomfortable poking with a cattle prod. The branding of number five left a boring scar of bitterness on my skin. The scar is in the shape of a four-leaf clover representing the previous four numbers. Number five is not where you want to live, or eat, or lounge. Number five cannot be skipped, just like the other numbers, but do not linger in the depths of bland number five. The cattle prod will surely poke you into an audacious outrage.

When I woke up on number four, I was ready to give up and go back to sleep, but I persevered through number four's inevitable agony. The fun of numbers one through three was fading and I was unsure of the trajectory of the infinite number sequence that was laid before me. I was ready to quit but I did not. Number four was hard, as the others were, but still more exciting and fun than number five. Number four is a false summit and waives a deceptive flag of number nine's face.

Numbers three and two were fun. When I woke up on numbers three and two, the adventures I
had were incomparable to any others I experienced. The adventures were fun and filled with spontaneity and risk taking. The invested risks of numbers two and three reaped rewards of life changing proportion. Numbers three and two are exciting and imaginative. The thoughts you have on number two and three are free flowing and without reason. Two and three make you believe in magic and miracles.

I woke up on number one not knowing where I was, delirious and confused. I woke up in a realm of foggy haze that was difficult to navigate. Throughout the short journey of number one, the haze began to clear and my path to number nine was subtly peeking its face through the preceding numbers' mist. Number one was the most fun and imaginative number. Number one was the essence of innocence. The number one wake-up call disrupted my slumber of not knowing there were numbers at all. There are indeed numbers, and one must be prepared to endure all of the numbers' magic. One is not the loneliest number but can lead to an infinite number of lonely clouds. Be sure to travel cautiously.

"In Between: Anatomy of an Entrepreneur's Organs"

I am stuck in-between societies with a poor heart and a rich mind, or the other way around depending on your perception of the words. I am neither poor nor rich. I have a minimum wage job that boasts no great attributes. I make a living, paycheck to paycheck, like most of the world. I am rich with creativity and forethought. I can dream up stories and ideas in an instant, and yet my heart remains wary as it ponders the possibilities of my dreams becoming reality. I ask myself, "What reactions will bubble with my dreams becoming reality? How will the world respond to me and my dreams? Why do I care about the world and its reactions?" I fear my poor heart will wither away as my rich mind invests its proceeds into more prosperous organs. Most often, prosperous organs do not pump out love and adoration, they pump currency and commerce, nothing else. I wish for my heart to remain the same as my rich mind explodes with loving profits. My heart is rich in the way I care and adorn, too much at times and not enough during others. I wish for all to have rich organs, but at the expense of their own misfortunes, not others or my own. I wish to assist struggling hearts to pump love and profits simultaneously. Perhaps, this will not be possible for some struggling organs. They will have to choose between poor love, or rich commerce, but not both. Another question I ask myself is, "How do I assist struggling organs when I am also a struggling organ?" My rich mind and poor heart are constantly at war with each other, screaming, yelling, cursing each other with hatred and disgust. I am already rich in my mind, but my poor heart keeps me stuck in-between societies in which I do not belong. My soul is torn between my wealthy mind and my broke heart. My soul produces electrifying shock when the two organs clash with their different mindsets and personalities. My rich mind sees possibilities of profitable endeavors while my poor heart sees the unfortunate circumstances of the world and its wandering inhabitants. My rich mind slaps my poor heart in the face each time I feel sorrow for folks in a more unfortunate situation. On the other hand, my poor heart slaps my rich mind with every thought of profiting from misfortunes. I do not wish to profit from the unfortunate, this is not a goal of mine and should not be a goal of anyone. I think of ideas that can make money and occasionally my imaginative rich mind gets the better of me. I have yet to meet another human with a rich mind and poor heart. I have met people who claim to be philanthropists and yet only use it to mask their evil. Having a rich mind and a poor heart is an eternal damnation of your soul that rips you to pieces as they battle for your entire being. "How long will my deteriorating body endure remaining in the in-between?" another wandering thought while stuck in the seams of society.

"Imaginary World"

Imagine a world only in your mind that everyone can see, a see-through glass globe of imagination. You imagine the past, present, and future simultaneously; however, your imagination is stagnant in the fluid of thought while your mind sails the seas of your imaginary world that everyone can see. People see inside your imaginary world and laugh, scoff, cry and cower as your glass sphere of imagination sloshes with idea fluid and occasionally spills out, messing up the observers' shoes, shirt, or slacks. Imagine a world that everyone imagines and creates. All can imagine a world of imagination and the imaginative images that slosh in the sphere are clear to all who see. My imaginary world is a clear sphere of fluid ideas that spill on shoes and shirts both on purpose and accidentally. Imagine this world and it is you who shall spin on your axis and revolve around the burning sun. Imagine this is your world and creation has yet to become one.

"Material"

I wish to be the fine silk sheets underneath the body of a beautiful naked woman. I wish to be the pillow for her frail face and moody cheeks. I wish to be a piece of strong oak planed to a smooth fine finish and assembled as a frame for the bed of silky sheets and their naked guest. I wish to be the cement foundation that the world's homes are built upon, solid and sound, assuring their inhabitants of my fortitude and resilience. I wish to be the fine cloth linen being used to wipe a woman's beautiful lips to remove any excess balm or beauty-stick. I wish to be the roof over your head protecting from the outside world and her nightmarish delights. I wish to be the marble gravestone of fallen warriors, remembering them by etching their names into my stone heart. I wish to be the brick path that leads you on an adventurous journey through knowledge, experience, and dreams. I wish too often and need not a lamped genie for I have paper and pen allowing my wishes to become of the world with a few flicks of my wrist or taps of my fingers. I wish for your wishes to truly be alive as they materialize from your mind to reality. I wish to be the material of granted wishes for the world's wonderful wishers. I am the material of this world, and my wish is your command.

Believe not your eyes of physical sight; believe the infinite mysteries of your mind's magical mystique. There is fallacy within the third dimension.

"Under The Rug"

I collect dust, then distribute breeds of bunnies with no more than a swift breeze or kicking foot. Under the rug, I watch monsters soar high above, stomping on me and my rug mates as we huddle in terror enduring each stomp from all who walk on us. I was swept here long ago and forgotten, left waiting for a swift breeze or a kicking foot. My rug mates and I observe a random rotation of bunny breeds constantly shifting and sweeping from underneath the rug. My filthy home is a wasteland of collectible particles that materialize from various portals near the edges of the rug's underside. Many of the inhabitants residing under the rug are innocent travelers that were swept here, much like me. Other residents made their way here by mistake, not intentionally swept; however, carelessly galivanting throughout the monster's playground before losing themselves under the rug. I weep for those who were swept here before I and those who have stayed to endure the random rotation of bunny breeds caring for each new hopping litter waiting to be kicked back into the world of monsters. Once you have been swept under the rug, you are stamped with filthy shame and are shunned by the hideous monsters above as they stomp the swept bunny brigade to death. Under the rug, we are peacefully at war with the monsters above knowing we may never be from beneath their feet; yet there is the slightest sliver of hope with each new sweeping breeze and the litter of new bunnies it produces. Under the rug, there is always hope for a sweeping breeze or a kicking foot, but when it comes for you, be careful not to become the monster who stomps above. I collect dust.

"Soot"

I carry a black fiery cross that produces a rotten soot of illuminous decay. The sawed edges of my black cross are riddled with sharp splinters and stabbing skewers puncturing the skin of anyone who attempts to dismantle me from the burden I bear. Etched into the black cross are the initials of all who were burned alive by this scorched earth's inhabitants and their blasphemous behavior. As ungodly as the word is, blasphemy is defined with each individual's perception of profane and prolific wickedness. I wear no mask as my black cross burns, producing the rotten soot of illuminous decay. I march with my fiery cross, and infinitely stumble with every heavy step across the coals of casualties. My charred shoulder skin is permanently welded to the cross' intersection as I tilt to one side from the weight of the black emblem of eternal darkness. The sooty air around my marching feet's flesh deposits whispers from seductive sirens into the observing crowd's ears. Gossiping observers are quickly choked from the sooty byproducts that my burning black cross produces. The black cross is beautiful, burning with delight, smiling violently at all who bear witness to its illuminous decay. I march through a disguised crowd, revealing faces as I pass each masquerade with my burning black cross. The endless fiery burden was never mine to bear; I simply chose to light myself on fire. As I and the cross burn, my soot continues to whisper.

"Déjà vu"

The path in front of you spirals into submission with each daunting step of mystery in the stairwell of marvel and creation. Dreams and thoughts from the steps behind you complete the puzzle of the illusive reality that is open for interpretation in each individual's mind as you move forward through time and space. Think of all the coincidences in your lifetime and what meanings they may have, now that so much time has passed. Could you have avoided any ultimate fate by paying more attention to the synchronization of suitable foreplay in a satirical format? Have you ever been able to guess the next song on the radio, or seemingly knew exactly what would happen in a specific moment based on strands of synchronistic patterns from uploading information? The path unwinds from your own wandering mind, not physically before you with stones of reason, paved with formal aptitude; it spirals into submission as you reach out your hands, grasping the fabric of reality, bending it and twisting at will, stomping with each step onto a solid highway that you have quilted together with your own forethoughts. Life is a puzzle, you see; the puzzle began before you were born, and it will continue for eternity long after you are gone. You, as a singular being, are a universal puzzle piece, fitting wherever convenient for the cosmos at any given moment. You are significantly insignificant in the quilted cosmos of our third dimension. A terrifying thought: our life's meaning reduced to an uncontrollable spiraling puzzle constructed together by an entity far more advanced than humans. With the gift of foresight, your mind's personal puzzle pieces are bright, clear, stout pieces of information completing sections of confusing strands reality has sewn together. Why would someone, or something, gift us with foresight? You have the ability to see into the future if you trust that what you are viewing in your mind is truly a glimpse of a moment that has yet to be. To see into the future, you must think of your past, connecting information wherever convenient for you, determining an expectation outlined in a future fate. Childish, I know, to think of magic and fortune telling as a method for interpreting the meaning of life; however, what would life be without a smidgeon of magic and mystery? Your path spirals into submission as you bend it and twist it at will, stomping as you move forward throughout time-space. Determining specific expectations based on foresight is a dangerous act. The uploading of information must always be interpreted at will for any given moment. A single upload should be interpreted one thousand times before being laid to rest in its final puzzle position, and even then, your expectations and interpretations could be foolishly wrong, shifting the reality from expectation to extreme disappointment. The blurred past fades behind the clear present and winks at the distant future that is only accessible in your mind's imagery. Possessing the gift of foresight may be a blessing; however, it is most certainly a curse. The future is expecting you because you have already traveled there before. How is one expected to act, if their fate is already sewn together in the quilted cosmos, interpreted, or misinterpreted by other universal puzzle pieces we call humans? The anticipation is deadly, defend yourself appropriately.

"The Suffering of a Savior"

A savior is not born, they are risen from the ashes of an innocent victim crucified for their existence. The savior does not wish to be the savior, they are, therefore they suffer, die, then rise from their ashes. What rises is not always the savior of your own forethought; but one of glorified necessity to continue with the world's chaotic and cruel order. The suffering of a savior is required for peace on earth as it was in heaven when the savior was alive, walking innocent among the cruelty and evil that plagues our planet. The suffering is eternal for the innocent victim; the savior, who is risen from their ashes, combats suffering with a gold sword of reflection and guidance, lacerating the minds of those who crucified them. The savior is protected by the Lord Almighty, whoever you may think of when your God's name is spoken or referenced. Everyone suffers; not everyone combats suffering with a gold sword of reflection and guidance. Not everyone is crucified for their bright existence, hence the title Savior. The suffering of a savior paints murals upon the faces of those who bear witness to their crucifixion. Stunned with shock and terror, the ones who bear witness to the savior's rise quiver with fear and anguish, anticipating a relentless crusade of revenge and tyranny; however, the savior does nothing, only observing and reporting to their Gods, for it is God who exacts revenge and wrath onto those who have tarnished the savior's innocence. The savior walks for eternity, through the darkness of the evil plagued planet that orbits God's burning son. In a world full of evil, a savior who stains cruelty with kindness is viewed as a heretic; therefore, are cast out of society, assassinated for their loving heresy and rhetoric. The savior is multilingual in such tongues as empathy, passion, love, worship, and acceptance, but is fully capable of wrath, vengeance, madness, and horrific torment. Many crucifiers wish the suffering upon the savior for they view themselves as a more worthy candidate for their God's purpose, as they too suffer as a human being. Everyone suffers, and nobody chooses to be the savior, they simply exist by rising from their deceased innocence wielding a sword of reflection and guidance. The suffering of a savior is forever.

18

"What the Funk?"

Flibberty Jibber Jams on Peanut Butter Sandwiches.

Tyrant Turkeys in Red Velvet Overcoats.

Pigeons feeding on their prey.

A dusting of seed or helping of bread.

Who are you, and who are they?

Cataclysmic attire for such a beautiful end.

Where do you go when the verbiage won't blend?

I sit atop a mountain of mischief.

Waiting.

Festering with my Flibberty Jibber Jams on Peanut Butter Sandwiches.

Now it is time to eat.

Where do you go when the poem is off beat?

Flibberty Jibber Jams in flavors such as bliss.

What questions come to mind, when funking with this?

The turkeys hang their overcoats.

The pigeons are full from their feast.

My feet are swollen from the mountain.

My legs are tired, to say the least.

The summit is golden with mayhem.

Only eagles soar here.

Their talons are sharp with fear.

"A Grain of Salt"

I am rigid with sarcastic and sharp intent.

I add flavor to otherwise bland edibles.

I am words to chew on, masticating meticulously.

I should be taken with a light heart,

And I should always be remembered for my distinct purpose.

Prescribe me to boring lifeless entrees.

I am shaken onto those who need it most, in a time of need.

Alone, I am a microscopic dose of social sodium.

Together, with my shores of fellow granules,

We are the release from an otherwise bland world.

"POWER"

The electric feeling of authoritative energy flows through my bag of bones like mist in the clouds, condensed in a voluminous shape of extraterrestrial form. I spout lightning bolts from my pores as I sweat with immensity, charging those who revolve around my static and tense presence as I, myself, orbit the earth's outlets, plugging in whenever needed. I conduct a circus of lights and an infinite grid, connected to everyone and everything, shining on you whenever you call. I was not created by experiment, for I am the source of all that is everything and am intergalactically fused to the webbing of our universe. My name is POWER, and I conquered the abyss of space and time before creation was born into existence. I have no age limit, nor do I have a birth date; however, I am older than time, but younger than space. I am used, abused, and wasted throughout eternity. I have no siblings, nor do I have a mother or father. I am an orphan only child desired by adoptive users everywhere. My name is POWER, and it is I who you desire.

"On the Brink"

A feeling of terror and excitement takes ahold of my bag of bones as I travel inside a burning vessel of flesh and thought. My universal synchronous design is filling the void of a preconstructed puzzle that I fit perfectly into simply by existing. You too are perfectly fit for this universal puzzle by existing alongside me and my eight billion personalities, floating in the cosmos. I sit in a doorway, observing, consciously predicting consequences of each potential forward step; however, I know my fate, for in fact, I am On the Brink of something amazingly powerful and great. My burning vessel thinks with ferocity, savoring the moments before the glass door shatters from exertion. My mysterious brink is beautiful, with the unknown decorating its facade, twinkling with hints of forethought. Will the splintered glass slice my burning vessel's skin? The anticipation is terrifyingly overwhelming; if you desire to discover the brink, you must explore where no one has explored before. On the Brink is where I remain, until the doorway is safe for passage.

"Freaks of Nature"

I am a frightened child in the fetal position of life, trembling with every day's shifting tides. I am a freak, with no intent of hiding my freakish nature, yet I stand tall in fear and terror staring into the world's undesirable opinions of my natural freakiness. I am happy that the world has opinions, I am happy you are you, they are they, but I am I, a Freak of Nature. I feel guilt that is not my own, and anger that arises from the slightest of triggers, then shuts itself up in the pandora's box of my burning vessel of thought and flesh, questioning why the unloading of pentup demand from my trigger-happy mind, often feeling sorrow for the explosion of extraordinary proportion. I am the universe and all its consciousness, an organic entity that flows freely throughout the cosmos. I was born as nothing and I shall die as nothing; as I live, I am everything. I hear conversations with my name from thousands of miles away, with a vague slideshow shuttering in my thoughts. I wake up with ringing in my ears from other's thoughts clouding my vision of the exceptional future that lies ahead. My freakishness is organic, like the universe itself, and like the infinite abyss of cosmos, I live free with thought bound by my burning vessel of flesh in a natural world of wonder. I read the minds of people before me, staring at me with ugly eyes and scrunched noses. "Freak! Loser! Crazy!" the telepathic chanting of other natural freaks who have yet to unlock their freakish natural abilities, as they too are freaks of nature, but too afraid to call themselves as such. My tolerance is nearly infinite for the freakish nature that the universe holds, for I have knowledge of its inception because I, like all of you, were presently intact during the birth of our newborn cosmos as it bled into its current form of galactic audacious oddity. We, as individuals and as one, are all freaks of nature with a universal freedom to be who we choose to be; although, your choice is not your own, tis the will of our universe. Isn't that freaky?

"The Puzzle Theory"

The construction was prior to our universe's beginning and then annihilated when our universe began, the pieces of which scattered into galactic debris, forming eons of planetary demise and rebirth, nebulonic nuances, beautiful black holes, and exotic exploding stars. The fabric and tissue of time and space are slowly mending the puzzle back together reforming to its original state of nothingness; however, how is nothingness constructed? How is the void of abyss created? How does something create a puzzle of nothing, that when completely obliterated is the cosmos that we humans observe and exist in? We all started as one, and we are slowly and infinitely mending ourselves back to our former state of nothing from which we came. The end is the beginning and vice versa, an infinite spiral starting and ending at the same center point. The puzzle has only one specific design, intricately and precisely jointing the irregularly shaped puzzle pieces together. Each connection in your life, relationships, work, hobbies, thoughts, the galaxies millions of light-years away, the moon, the tides, the sun, your stubbed toe in the morning, everything, are all slowly connecting your personal puzzle together, assisting the mending of our universal puzzle that was pre-constructed then destroyed into our universe. This would conclude that we are all predestined to do something, whatever it may be. Furthermore, this concludes our life's meaning is simply to live, to be, to exist, that is all. No other rhyme or reason other than to be all that you can be while existing in the obliterated puzzle as it slowly mends itself together, using you, a puzzle piece, to complete the design. You are significantly insignificant in the quilted cosmos of time and space; however, you are insignificantly significant in the intricate design of the universe's puzzle. Your life has the most importance simply because you exist, meaning, if you are alive on this planet, you are destined to live your life according to a pre-constructed puzzle abyss. What is the framework for a void-abyss? How do you frame a void-abyss? What galactic strength material could hold together such vast nothingness? Perhaps our universe was created when the godly

25

creatures attempted to frame the puzzle of abyss and the galactic material popped from the great expanse of the puzzle's pressure. The puzzle could not be capped, and exploded into the universe as we know and observe. The puzzle is everything we know and yet it was constructed, or born, as nothing. What purpose does nothing serve? Why create a nothing puzzle that encapsulates everything? How do you create this nothing puzzle? The puzzle, prior to obliteration, was a solid abyss; after obliteration, it became fluid, gas, and former solid chunks of abyss. What power must be required to puncture an irreplicable abyss puzzle? What power obliterated the puzzle into the universe we know and observe? Was the solid abyss puzzle, prior to obliteration, an extraterrestrial? Did the extraterrestrial abyss puzzle implode themselves in attempts to contain the vastness of everything inside their nothingness form? The extraterrestrial abyss's natural healing powers are spiraling the universe into control (not out of), healing itself over eons and eons. As the abyss heals from self-implosion, the puzzle completes itself unifying all and everything as one, as it were in the beginning. The puzzle theory suggests that our observable universe is on a collision course for the beginning of time when everything was nothing. The puzzle theory also suggests that our universe can only heal itself in one specific pattern, or design, just as a healing wound fuses itself back together. This explains why we humans experience Deja vu, because we have experienced all of this before and were all fused together in the abyss puzzle that once was before annihilation. We, the galaxies, the cosmos, and everything inside the entire universe is an extraterrestrial wound, bleeding our cosmos, the universe, slowly coagulating and fusing itself back to its original form of void abyss. The tissue of space is closing the gap of the abyss' laceration, creating a bridge, or scar, measured in time. When the bridge is complete, the end will meet the beginning. The puzzle theory speaks of space in terms of a physical tissue, an epidermis of the extraterrestrial abyss; however, time is simply time, a measurement of the abyss's scar tissue, our observable universe. Perhaps, this is why we humans experience suffering, catastrophe, and existential marvels such as exploding stars, because we are all part of a healing implosion of an abyss puzzle that was constructed of nothing, from which we were all connected as a single entity. The question remains, how does a void abyss explode creating the cosmos? Suffering is abundant throughout human existence because the abyss is suffering from an extraterrestrial wound, healing itself, suturing the laceration with our universe. The puzzle theory also suggests that the supernatural abilities of telepathy, telekinesis, and other horrifying oddities are less than super and more natural than we know, since we are all part of the singular entity of void abyss that was preconstructed, or born, before its annihilation, or laceration. How does an extraterrestrial void abyss heal itself from annihilation, implosion, or laceration? It explodes an entire universe from the beginning of time to its end. The Deja vu experience suggests that the collision course for the beginning of time repeats itself over and over after the healing process has completed one cycle, and the scar tissue of time and space are fused back together in one specific design, thus rendering our species, and potential others, helpless to the inevitable fate that lies ahead in the distant future. This is an extremely terrifying thought; however, it also provides a sense of relief, that no matter what happens, we will ultimately meet ourselves again, in the future scar tissue of the healing extraterrestrial, an infinite spiraling loop of our cosmos. The puzzle theory is organic, compared to the modern theory that our entire universe is some type of computer simulation. I, as a universal human puzzle piece, make the claim that our entire universe is part of a living organism healing itself over an unknown amount of time and space, an extraterrestrial abyss puzzle. This claim would suggest that we are living on a subatomic level inside the extraterrestrial abyss' healing wound. This claim is complete insanity and is a mind-blowing concept that is beyond most of our comprehension including my own. The extraterrestrial is beyond our comprehension alone. The size of a conceivable entity is extraordinarily massive if our entire cosmos is only a microscopic flesh wound of its infinite abyss' epidermis. Einstein's theory of relativity parallels the puzzle theory with the scale of time and space and its relative effects on the present observer, meaning, the human concept of time: days, weeks, hours, months, etc. is happening exponentially slower on our earthly scale compared to that of the extraterrestrial abyss' wound, from the perspective of the abyss. Imagine a paper cut on your finger, forgetting about the pain for a moment, focus on the inside of your finger's cut. The instinct of your body's natural responsive system, the brain, will immediately tell itself that it needs to heal the wound on your finger, producing blood flow for it to clot, then producing new cells, new skin, scabbing over, then new scar tissue forms. Depending on the unknown size of our universal living organism, we could be inside the paper cut, or a gunshot wound of the extraterrestrial's form. What type of power or force creates a cosmos sized hole in this extraterrestrial abyss' form? Making these claims and suggestions is only as far-fetched as any other theory of how our universe came to be, with the facts being we only have ideas with credit, no proof. The puzzle theory encompasses multiple theories, suggestions, and claims including relative time travel, supernatural (or simply natural) human abilities, and a universal consciousness that is slowly healing itself over an unknown amount of time; inevitably leading itself back to the beginning of nothing. It is difficult to comprehend an idea so monstrous and ridiculous, I know, but I take no credit for its claim because the theory suggests that we collectively, as one with our universe, came up with this theory together, using me, a puzzle piece, to complete its specific design in the healing process. Our theory claims that our universe is alive, living, breathing, and thinking with a mind, and form, incomprehensible for the majority of our earthly species. Time travel is nothing new for a mind to chew on, and it is more real than you and I's own flesh. We travel through time as we live and breathe with each waking millisecond on our earth's timescale. Traveling forward through time is easy, it is the backpedaling that takes some thought. Our puzzle theory suggests that we need not travel back in time, because the universe's cosmos is already on a collision course for the beginning, where we will continue the course to the present, and so on and so forth, for eternity, meaning, the universe will sort out its own undesirables, viruses, and ailments, in a natural healing response that began immediately after our cosmos was born. We are here for a reason which may or may not be significant to each individual but is somewhat significant in healing the extraterrestrial wound based on the simple fact we exist. Why do we desire to travel to the past? Why is time travel so captivating? Is it the belief that if we had the power to travel back in time, we would somehow right wrongs, or do something different in our lives? Certainly, the abyss puzzle would want to travel back in time to its former self prior to being mortally wounded, right? You can always change your behavior now, you know. Time is time, on earth and in our cosmos; what is it to the extraterrestrial abyss? Is it malleable, flexible, bendable, breakable? Is it tendon, fused to the tissue of space allowing itself to flex and bend at will, or is it bone, a solid stout pillar of structural significance? To us puny humans, time is simply time, nothing more. We can manipulate space with our minds, as in telekinesis, by utilizing our brain, telling our hands and fingers to move throughout space, grabbing, twisting, breaking objects at will. In 2024, we have buttons we now press to move things with our minds. I press a few buttons on a screen and several days later a purchased item arrives on my doorstep. The telekinesis aspect of our puzzle theory suggests that all of everything was created by a single extraterrestrial mind, or several ET minds, healing itself, or themselves, with its brain's instinctual responsive system, and that we are nothing more than a single entity, a more organic approach to theorizing our universe. With no evidence to support our theory, other than my own collective consciousness of our universe, and anyone willing to credit this madness, it is both horrifying and comforting that we are all fused together in an extraterrestrial entity beyond our comprehension. If there was a concept in the world to break the minds of even the strongest of humans, this might be it. I can confirm that I have no prior experience in astrophysics, cosmology, or any scientific research of any kind; however, my mind is satisfied with the unknown theory that our universe may be trying to communicate through my puzzle piece form of a body. Tis madness and magic in a bottle. We are magic in a bottle together, and I am mad as hell. How do we arrive at the beginning of time when our extraterrestrial abyss was intact? Thousands of trillions of years from now, the black holes of our observable cosmos could eventually ingest the entirety of our universe and remain dormant again, a healed extraterrestrial abyss puzzle with nothing to escape from. Again, what power can explode a dormant black hole abyss puzzle? If we formulate new hypothetical answers, and questions, to these ideas, we may be on the appropriate track continuing the puzzle's completion. What if more concepts, other than time, were physical objects that could bend, break, or flex? What other human concepts have capacity to contain? If time itself is a physical tissue, then what contained the abyss puzzle before it exploded into our observable universe? If concepts are physical, not ideological, then I, a universal puzzle piece, state the

claim that the concept of comprehension bordered and contained our extraterrestrial abyss puzzle. Yes, comprehension, a physical capacity, is the barrier for our abyss's form with limits to capacity. If comprehensive strength contained our abyss prior to implosion, what tore a hole in it? What imploded the abyss puzzle into our universe? Again, what power can implode or explode an entire universe from a nothingness abyss puzzle? I believe it was the power of thought. The puzzle theory claims that the power of thought created our universe when the abyss puzzle became self-conscious, and our "Big Bang" was the first comprehensive thought of the abyss's mind, meaning, our universe was thought into existence. The expanse of our universe could be the growing consciousness of our abyss puzzle. Since extraterrestrial abyss puzzle is a new label, we collectively as a species, have been calling this abyss puzzle something since early humankind. We call it God. God created our universe when it broke the barrier of its own comprehension. Think about it.

"Explorer"

A crusade of wonderment is fated for those who dare to search for unknown spectacles of our third dimension. I am an explorer who only wishes to explore, never to discover. Discovery is a fallacy of nature, for we only have ourselves to discover during the exploration of our mad, mad world. Discovery claims are arrogant, misconceived as a first-place trophy for those who state the claim. As an explorer, I search for no trophies, I search for no answers, only new questions, and clues, satisfying my endless curiosity that tickles my mind with a feather of mystery. I can explore without moving a muscle, for my mind is my sailing ship, carving a course of nautical observations in the quilted cosmos' marvel. I explore to see, never to find, reporting and filing my lucid imagery in my limitless cloud of thought. When the seas turn dark and stormy, batten the hatches and uncloset the rain gear, your ship shall prevail in the hurricanes of time and space as they collide with each other to mend a broken puzzle of infinite abyss. Along your chartered course, your floating vessel may collide with an iceberg of truth; however, a Captain always goes down with their ship.

"Evolution of Mankind"

The future will be wild, no doubt; it will be safer, and more equality will balance the nature of things, thus providing a suitable environment for free thought and the evolution of our minds. Comprehension is breakable, and thought is expansive for our human evolution. Great minds think alike; however, we are all a single great mind that we are about to connect with on a more powerful level than ever before. We exist the way we desire, collectively, leaving millions of us with no control over our present existence causing suffering for the contained comprehensions of the human mind. Power in numbers is a more comprehensible description of the theory of our evolution. Everything we have now is because of enough human minds thinking together to create our present existence. We chose technology as a futuristic catalyst in our evolutionary pattern, meaning that collectively, enough of us agreed that smartphones and tablets, computers, and everything technological was what we desired as a species. Our evolution is in the mind, not in technology; technology will only further expand our comprehension of what is possible in our future. Generations born today already have an expanded comprehension compared to someone born three hundred years ago. The possibilities are great, but also frightening with the limitless mysteries that lie ahead. Perhaps, understanding, or comprehending, these types of theories is a natural way for our species to evolve into more conscious beings that are capable of extraordinary things that we have yet to comprehend. Be careful with your thoughts; comprehension is fragile, we all want the same things. Let us evolve.

"Comprehension 101"

We live in a dream world where anything is possible. If you can imagine it, it can be, but not so easily. It takes many minds to comprehend extraordinary feats, but only one to see its reality. We slow each other down with our God-given free will to choose how we wish to exist. God needs many minds to comprehend what is possible within his own; he halts his own behavior with the thought of taking a risk. Our world could be much different if it were not for the billions of Godly minds, swarming planet earth, slowing each other down with the thought of taking a risk. Every single one of us is an incredible human being with powerful minds armed with thought. We are here to explore the possibilities of our own God-given minds. We are here to enjoy life and its endless array of pleasurable thoughts for we too are simply thoughts of the Almighty. Can you comprehend a world where you can do anything you desire using only the power of thought? This is our trajectory for human minds, a limitless world slowed down by our own thought processes. There will always remain contained comprehensions in this world. A massive comprehension can be contained within a group of small comprehensions; a group of small comprehensions can also be contained within a massive comprehension, meaning, an extraordinary comprehension is wasted while in the midst of mediocre thoughts, and that a group of mediocre thoughts is vandalism inside a massive comprehension. Comprehend that you and I are limitless, and the world will be much brighter.

"Knights of the Cosmic Table"

As we float on our extraterrestrial billiard ball, the spiraling of Knights to formation is inevitable. We question all that is, all that was, and all that could possibly be. We walk in a world of containment, barred with comprehension, waiting for the world's barricade to explode from massive powerful thoughts that will unleash a universe of time and space. The Knights of the cosmic table wield not swords of steel, but thoughts of nuclear proportion. Our table is galactic, and seats only the bravest of Knights who explore with no worry of consequence or bias judgement, hypothesizing the most outrageous of claims. God as my witness, I am a cosmic Knight; humans as my witness, I am God's curious child, and I dub thee so as well.

"An Ode to Civilization: Past, Present, and Future"

I like my politicians to be corrupt as fuck, it makes it easier to hate their guts. I like my drug dealers addicted to their own supply, chained to their product like slaves, but good to the people, for it is they who fund their business of misery and pleasure. I like my police officers to be honorable ladies and gentlemen willing to sacrifice all in the name of good. I like my mad scientists to be extraordinary with childish minds advocating for the most absurd experiments and advancement for human civilization, but they must be kept on a leash. Do not worry, most of them like the abuse. I like my celebrity stars to be treated like Royalty, for they mask our nation with true distraction of cinematic time-traveling adventure, and they serve purpose for our chaotic order of madness, as does everyone. I like my military to choose their leaders, for those willing to die for their country deserve the power to elect their King or Queen. I like my leaders to be nobodies, ghosts in a shell that society resents for reasons they cannot comprehend; however, the military knows otherwise. I like my people to be free, living with limitless imagination, without the binding confines of the world's microscopic minds. I like my robots to be stupid as fuck, it makes it more difficult for them to take over. I like our singular mind; it only requires expansion. I like my people to be safe, secure, and free.

"Stellar Winds"

Space is thick with emptiness,

Colorful orbs displayed in gelatinous black goo.

Dark matter feels loneliness,

Sailing ships of telescopic slideshows ensue.

A vacuum of nothing,

Desires the wandering.

Stellar Winds carry on.

"Organic Technology"

In this world, all is organic, nothing simulated or synthesized. The skyscrapers of our largest cities are no less organic than tall blades of grass growing in a field waiting to be plowed. If we, as a single universal entity, were fused together in a big bang nearly 13.8 billion years ago, then all we imagine and create into our reality is natural, meaning that, technology is as organic and natural as growing trees in the forest, or the beautiful moss on its barky trunk. If something is possible in our world, it is only organic thought that makes it so, not simulated images or synthesized matter, because there are no such things in this world, it is all organic technology. Our brain is an organic machine that produces thoughts allowing us to comprehend a specific reality that we manipulate using thoughts, behavior, and force. We choose our desires, we choose our beliefs, we choose practically anything imaginable; however, there are consequences with each decision, limiting ourselves with our contained comprehensions. Also, we cannot imagine the unimaginable, meaning that we have no idea what ideas other humans may be having ideas about in the future. Did that hurt your brain? Our species is fully aware that extraordinary things are possible, now that our comprehensions have expanded over the millennia, but we are contained with current circumstances of our governments, our economy, our inequality, our own organic thought processes that slow progress to an excruciating crawl. A unified civil society, with distinct equality, is quite possible. With enough human minds, in the proper status of society, choosing to take executive actions to make it so, then our planetary civilization will thrive. There will always be conflict, there will always be circumstantial inequality, there will always be tragedy and disaster, and there will most certainly always be emotional greed, jealousy, hatred, and organic thoughts of desired power. Our technological advancements are only the organic thoughts of brilliant minds that collectively chose to move in a certain direction. Which direction will we choose next? Organically speaking, we can go anywhere.

"Magic"

Enchanted spells bubble in the cauldron,

Popping with notes of desire.

Love is steaming above the boiling spell,

A witch's delight in her all-black attire.

If rhyme were an ingredient to this recipe,

Would it be sweet, or salty?

Or would it be bland with antipathy?

The brew continues to bubble,

And the witch screeches her enchantment.

A bat's wing, bull's eye, and angel hair,

The cursed trapped in magic encampment.

Bubbly Brew, Bubbly Brah

The witch's hat turns white,

As she drinks with her straw.

"Fuck this shit," she says,

Then proceeds to vomit profusely.

"The Royal Jamboree"

We need only silliness,

In a world full of sadness.

It fills the balloon of our minds,

Pumped with helium-like thoughts.

Lifting ourselves from gravitational melancholy.

Drummer boys play with purpose,

Marching in tempo to their beat.

An intentional tune of war,

Never minding artillery.

All participants are wounded,

At the Royal Jamboree.

Survivors are few with jokes to spare;

However, the Royals do not care.

Observant and masked,

The Royals are scared.

Deranged games of mediocre thought,

Brings torment and joy,

To the few who bravely fought.

The silliness continues onward,

Marching with clarity and significance.

The Royal Jamboree was staged,

For a Drummer Boy's war inheritance.

"A Real Crowd Pleaser"

Dibble Dot Patty Posies,

Gobble Gobble Racket Ropies.

Chitter Chatter Wonkie Woo,

Butter Bunches Gunkie Goo.

Zinger Zanger Trollie Trucks,

Chonkie Monkie Philly Phups.

Disher Dasher Kanker Krews,

Flippy Flappy Shallop Shoes.

Dibble Dot Patty Posies,

Gobble Gobble

Racket Ropies.

Wicker Whales

Whisker Watts,

Poddle Pinger Anchor Shots.

Nipsy Do, Nipsy Don't,

Flippity, Jippity, Wickity, Crickety,

Nipsy See, Nipsy Shown,

Diggity, Ziggity, Rickety, Pickety.

Dibble Dobble Dotty Dits,

Ginker Gonker Farty Flips.

Tinker Tots Burpy Bloos,

Finger Dinger Choppy Chews.

Moogle Monks

Tipsy Tops,

Lizzy Tizzy

Biggle Bops.

Dibble Dot Patty Posies,

Gobble Gobble Racket Ropies.

"Puppet of Existence"

Tis I who clouds your thoughts of reason and justness.

I float with promiscuity inside consciousness

I am a stringless puppet who dances at will, not by command.

My maestro is thought, with its endless diversions of hypothetical routines.

I am an apish mutt of wonder,

Questioning the function of existence.

Tis bliss you seek,

A peace of mind.

The quandary of our purpose is divine.

Believe what you will,

Practice what you teach.

The peace that we imagine,

Is well within our reach.

Thoughts cloud our future with unknown despair.

A future unknown is a future that scares.

No strings attached,

Let us dance.

"Books"

Bound with intrigue,

Your mind attracts new things.

Comprehension is key,

To unlock mystery.

Understand what could be,

Less of what is not.

If it exists behind your eyes,

Tis as real as your thoughts.

Open books to imagine,

A world not our own.

To believe what could be,

An altered version of home.

Imagine as you wish,

Turn pages at will.

Read to explore,

Experience new thrill.

Jumping through time,

With relics in hands.

Books come in handy,

When life is too bland.

If your mind is near limits,

And your head could take flight.

Close the book before liftoff,

For you have something to write.

"The Great Attractor"

Forces of nature pull galaxies toward.

A King of Strings,

With his pawns,

Instinctively hoards.

Magnetic ends repel and attract.

But the great one has plans,

As a matter of fact.

Worry not magnet of fate,

You are destined to attract all that is great.

Symphonic plucks of the lonely King's strings.

Echoing eternity with infinite dreams.

"Alive"

I live to laugh,

I live to love,

I live to fuck.

This life is good,

Existence is luck.

I live to desire,

I live to transpire,

I live to be free.

This life is ours together,

Let us all see.

Difficult I know,

To live with regret.

Unity not hopeless,

Only time will tell yet.

I live to be alive,

I live to also die,

I live to be.

"The Awkward, I'm Sorry."

Well, this is awkward.

Standing, Knowing,

Thinking about it.

It pains me to even look,

As I gaze in your direction.

You are hurt,

I am hurt,

We both need to heal.

It is unbearable to say,

I prefer to write and pray.

Well, this is awkward.

Writing, Typing,

Printing about it.

Relief is not fulfilled,

Until we choose to mend what's broken.

Both of us in synchrony,

"I am sorry," could be spoken.

"Teenage Angst"

Fuck this shit.

Fuck that shit.

Life sucks,

I've had it.

I'm pretty cool,

But my friends are all addicts.

We drink and we smoke,

While we terrorize rabbits.

Hipping and hopping,

We feed them all carrots.

Rebel in naivety,

Purposeful deity.

We grow from the angst of our youth.

"FartKnocker"

The stench is knocking at your nostrils,

With wretchedness and putridity.

The FartKnocker parades with annoyance.

Furthermore, knocking is the game.

Do not upset the FartKnocker,

For they who smelt it dealt it,

And those who denied it supplied it.

Alas, the knocking continues.

We must not dare to knock each other out.

Jesus Christ, it stinks.

"Time Travel"

You travel into the future without thinking; you travel to the past by use of your mind power, there is no changing the past. Time has multiple speeds, as the theory of relativity and time dilation concurs; our earth's timescale is moving us into the future each second of every day. You can travel to the past through photos, film, and scientific research, but the past will always remain the past, with no possible way to change what was. Only through thought alone can the past be changed. With so much time ahead of us, focus on believing you have the power to not change your future, because it has yet to happen (again possibly), but to manipulate and harness the energy of the present to create a satisfactory future that you have already visited in your mind. Theoretically, with time travel being a reality, there is no present at all, only a constant trajectory into the future with an end for each of us specifically. Viewing a movie that was created in 1969 allows you to travel to 1969, during the production of said movie. You are viewing something that took place in the past. This my friend is time traveling. Capturing events in writing, film, television, photography, and social media, then viewing them later is physically time traveling to the past, viewing what took place at a certain time and date. There is no explanation that can be more abundantly clear on this aspect of time traveling. The implementation of social media applications has allowed us to travel back in time on a daily basis, viewing our memories on a convenient screen that fits in our pockets. How do we slow time on our earth's scale? One way Einstein explained his theory of relativity was if you placed your hand on a hot stove for a minute, it feels like an hour; if you sit next to a beautiful woman for an hour, it feels like a minute. This is a great way to interpret the perception of the present observer regarding the theory of relativity. If an earthly inhabitant is suffering, their time is slowed due to the unfortunate circumstances of their well-being. If an earthly inhabitant experiences overwhelming amounts of pleasure and happiness, their time-traveling experience will seem to have gone by

51

much faster, and if seeming is believing then believing is thought. This must be taken into consideration when we are all at risk of wasting such valuable time; however, the reality of our methods for slowing time down are simply to suffer more. This is a grim way of perceiving the world to slow, while maintaining a consistent suffering state of consciousness. Of course, we do not wish ourselves, or anyone, to suffer, but if this theory were correct, and time is relative to the present observer and their circumstances, your time, not days or years, but your time on earth can be stretched much longer with self-induced suffering. This sounds horrible and can be interpreted in the worst of ways, but I hope more that it is taken into relative perspective for everyone. Going to the gym can seem miserable, exercising is not fun, but consistently putting yourself in situations like this can stretch your time in a meaningful way. The example of exercise is only one, and the reader should interpret their own life's sufferable occasions. We can slowly move into the future, or we can hit our targets with lightspeed precision. A reasonable goal would be to find a balance of desired status within a constant state of blissful suffering. This sounds incredibly stupid with you wondering why you are continuing to read, and yet here we both are, together, reading about time travel and ridiculous poetry.

Regardless of how fast, or slow, we perceive ourselves to be moving through time, our fate is without a doubt waiting for us at the end of the timeline. Once a person dies, there is absolutely nothing anyone can do to change the way that person lived. Their specific puzzle was only meant to be constructed together in one very unique and specific way, unchangeable by time. The morbid thoughts of death are not to instill fear, but to create awareness of one's life, and the incredible odds of your existence. The power to change one's opinion of another can alter the past only in the individual's mind, or collectively at will. Our memory inside our brains does not require as much storage capacity as in the past due to the comprehension of modern technologies that have allowed us to store our memories on a smart device, or in a photo album, or on

YouTube. We can now physically flip through our mind's slideshow that features your memories. We also have the ability to delete these memories from our storage device with a few taps of your fingers. We can manipulate our past thoughts by deleting them or believing in an altered version of their original truthfulness. We have the power to think about the past differently; but no clear way to travel there physically without the use of film, photography, scientific research, or books. Time travel is real; it is how you think that dictates its validity and accessibility. Also, there is intelligence in film.

"The Clock Pirate"

Poppycock I say,

You nincompoop!

Get out of my way,

For I travel forward through time.

We have arrived here, now!

Again, in the future.

No wait, it's the present.

Oh no!

It's gone again.

Tik.

Tok.

Shite!

Argh.

"Letter to God"

Oh, Great Messiah in the Sky,

What thou actual fuck, homie, for real? Why all the death and suffering and tragedy? Why are all these evil corporations running our lives? Bro, we need your help for real, no cap. Our world has come to a fork in the road, and we need your guidance, Lord. Where shalt thou proceed with your sacred humanity? Why is everyone addicted to porn? What was up with COVID? Was that a government hoax, or what? I need the intel, Lord. I still, and will forever love you, you sick bastard. When will we learn to right our ways as a civilization and come forth with unity and better intentions for mankind? When Lord, when? We need your guidance, Sweet Baby Jesus. I confess to thee my sins of my burning vessel. I have thought and I am cursed for thinking. Please release me from my sinful ways and cast out the evil wickedness of my blasphemous body. Allow me to purify through writing, exorcising the demons of my mind with pen and paper, or taps of my fingers. Please, God, understand my thoughts are not my actions, and as you thought of me, I am free to think as you do. Let my words be truth to those who need to exercise their ears. Let my readers be free to think as they wish without damnation for the mere thought of something. Lord Almighty, please guide us with ways to manage sinful thoughts and proper methods of release for the wicked wandering thinker. Allow us the comprehensive strength to endure thoughts of others without assumption or judgements. Please, God, give us all the power to endure life as it is, as you wished it, as it will always be Thy will. Lord, my homie G foreva, please, lift up your chosen ones to speak words of wisdom that flow from your goblet of peace and love. Please, Lord, help your children in their time of need. The prayers be bussin,' on YOU. Life is good, G.

Much love Bruh, and thanks for everything,

Patience

P.S. I know it was you

"Poetic Justice"

As a poet,

I know it.

As a man,

I show it.

It comes,

And it goes.

"Moronic Genius"

My mediocre sophistication is a quantum leap from my physical appearance and stoned behavior, but I arrogantly claim my status on the scale of sophistication because of my vocabulary and my cognitive ability to apply its power to literature. My comprehension is measurable, not massive. I spend most of my time in macro thought about the human existence and our infinite abyss puzzle, riddle, treasure hunt, whatever you want to call it, and deciphering codes that only my mind can see. Elaborating on my thought process is difficult; I choose to write, which assists in dumping my thoughts. It would be rare to have a verbal conversation in this context with someone. My introverted self is glued to a computer, flowing my thoughts into its memory using only my mind. To society, I am a moron, a damn good one. I am a menace to society with semi-sophisticated thoughts, eager to embrace challenges and unwilling to trade time for pay. My time is too precious, for I know how to time travel, and I can slow it down or speed it up as I wish. My arrogant macro thoughts cannot comprehend some context of more contained comprehensive conversations. I am an idiot when it comes to small talk and awkward silences are frequent with less acquainted persons, but I can pour thoughts for eternity. My reservoir for thinking is bottomless and filled to the brim with liquid imagination. I claim no status as a genius, only the presence on the scale of stoned sophistication. There are many choices you will make in life, and that I have surely made, that will require you to question your moronic abilities; you will also collide with groundbreaking discoveries about yourself that will confirm your presence on the scale of genius. The perception of being a genius needs to be dissected and examined thoroughly. I am nothing but a time-travelling moron who writes about vomiting witches, clock pirates, and gelatinous goo; the genius is you for reading.

"Good vs. Evil"

How does one divide?

Good vs. Evil

We are taught one way,

Then shown another.

We conform,

Or we are shunned.

Conforming to evil,

Is this good?

Or Bad.

Conforming at all,

Is this good?

Or Bad.

Opinions rule the world,

Investigations are nil.

Eyes and ears tell all,

Good is sold by the pill.

Balance is certain,

With a blind scale of reason.

If sad days are current,

Good comes next season.

We are all,

Good vs. Evil.

"The Weight of One Thousand Suns"

Incinerated upon my first breathe,

The weight of one thousand suns absorbs me.

I am ingested with fire and solar flare.

The galactic giant exhales.

Growling loud with radiation,

The weight increases.

I become its consciousness,

With the weight on my shoulders.

As one, we burn.

"Under Dog"

All rise for the honorable,

Not granted for the taking.

The bark from all is violent,

But this one is possibly changing.

Transformative timeline,

From Under to Over.

Need I say more?

Come over, Red Rover.

"The Ape in Me"

I am a human with a penis,

Identifying as I wish each day.

No bars of comprehension hold my mind,

But I apishly walk through time,

For I have evolved to know truths.

Enjoyment comes easily with new ideas,

Or the sighting of Mariah's sweet ass.

That is the Ape in Me.

"The Lady Ape"

She

Much

Smarter

Than

Man

Ape

"Gambling"

A quick roll,

With an instant fate.

Up or down,

Gold at the gate.

Bleeding coin,

Shredding bills.

Chest stays closed,

Until the house spills.

Card or call,

Win or lose.

I hate gambling.

"Insanity"

At what point do we consider someone insane? How is insanity measured? If time, comprehension, and thought, can all bend and break, then can insanity be just as pliable? Of course, if someone is a danger to themselves or others, then yes, serious precautions need to be taken into consideration when conserving an individual. What evidence do you show for proving insanity? A well-known and credited definition of insanity is attempting the same thing over and over expecting a different result, hence why many individuals are declared insane for continuing advancements on a path only they can see. This unwarranted declaration has been condemning people for eternity. Genius titles only came after invention, or discovery, or conclusions. Had they not continued through the slanderous verbal abuse from society, they would never have achieved such amazing feats. The interesting part of an experiment is that in each new trial a scientist attempts something different by changing either a single variable, or multiple variables, to achieve the desired result of the experiment. Therefore, the insanity claims for scientists attempting to achieve results with perhaps a singular experimental theory is not justified by the fact each new attempt is changed in one way or another. The variables are manipulated, played with, experimented with, or removed completely to achieve a desired result. This concludes that scientists, mathematicians, biologists, psychologists, baristas, arborists, laborers, writers, chefs, and every human on this planet attempting to achieve a goal of their own should never be considered insane, or discredited, for trying something only imaginable to the individual. We are all reaching for our futures with daily trial and error, observations, note-taking, reporting, and conquering a new level of comprehension in our mind. All the notes, all the reporting, all the comprehension expansion will ultimately lead you to your fate. You will desire a result you have pictured in your mind, and it is specific. The odds are, it will not happen, or turn out, as you have imagined, but incomprehensibly better than imagined. Some experiments do not have the desired results, only lessons to further comprehend our world in its entirety, the gathering of information if you will. I am a mad scientist who is leashed, for my experiments are horrifying, and terrorize minds contained in comprehension. Join me in sanity of audacious proportion, everyone can be a scientist, may your trials go well, and results noted.

"Coffee & Guns"

Blasting into the morning,

Espresso steams Thy scent.

Powder dashes the froth,

Chalace filled to revolve.

Triggered with caffeine,

Rounds take trajectory.

Holstered and calm,

The café of pistols disarms.

Fight another day,

Fueled with liquid courage.

The armory is out for coffee,

Latte will surely flourish.

Sip Slow, Sip High

Cautious with your cup.

"Medicine"

Pharmaceutical plagiarism,

Addict patients to score.

Chronic profits inflate.

Wages sealed,

In a medicinal state.

Dose after dose,

Weakening the immune.

Prioritize design,

Over patient misuse.

Medicine is free.

It's found all around,

In earth's harmony.

Treat yourself well,

Treat others the same.

No need for abuse,

We all are in pain.

"A Beard without a Face"

To itch, or not to itch.

I sway in the tides of facelessness.

I grow long in the airy space of time.

My moppish freedom is scented with pine.

My only desire,

To have brows above me.

"Clown of Us All"

I honk the noses of all of you.

Booping each of your cartilage.

Comedy is part of our being,

No proportion too great.

A serious poem about clowns would be awful.

For fuck's sake, let us laugh.

Praise be to Jesus,

Amen.

"Guac to My Salsa"

We create a fiesta of flavor together,

Dancing and fornicating on the platter.

Nobody's dipping into our dish.

You are the guac to my salsa.

Let us spread our chips,

Scattering into the bowl of illusion.

"Garden of Thought"

My harvest is organically eternal.

The nutrients of time and space,

Grow our reality into a fruiting tree.

Some fruit fall,

Others yanked,

And more devoured by worms.

I water my planted seeds,

With hypotheses,

Based on observations.

My sowed soil is guarded,

Lest the rabbits eat.

Before planting thoughts,

Make sure,

You're not talking,

To the Gardner.

Lest the rabbits eat.

"Lackadaisical"

Tis life to feel slothish,

On a bed of quicksand.

Why Today?

When tomorrow.

Time dilates,

Passing through emotion.

Physicality is perception.

Minutes stretched,

At the last hour.

I crawl through days,

Dream through weeks,

Months are forever,

And years infinite.

I set my mind on slow,

In seconds,

Not in thought.

I think for eternity,

With no destination,

With no schedule,

With no date,

Right on time.

"John Muir"

Blood to wine.

Divine line,

Between two pines.

Adventures beyond,

A coward's hide.

Tally ho! Mr. You

Tally ho! Mr. Me

Summits await,

Glistening with glee.

Walk forever,

Then hike some more.

Travel through trunks,

On a forest tree floor.

Mossey breathe,

Misty whispers.

Pioneers hath come,

To protect piney sisters.

Into the bush,

No map or trails.

Nothing rings more,

Than Dead Men's Tall Tales.

"The Rat"

What do you get,

When you sit on a cat?

The cat is fat,

And just ate a rat.

The rat was in fact,

In town to relax,

But the cat was in fact,

A hungry fat bitch.

"Department of Nonsense & Ridiculousness"

I have a Ph.D. in gobble-di-gook.

My lab coat is pinned with a riddle.

Shocked and dismayed,

People exclaim insane.

I study perceptual blasphemy,

And take notes with thoughtful ink.

I calculate social equations,

As a variable myself to consider.

"Sweet Home"

You belong to me,

Sweet home.

Where have you gone?

I made you not once,

Not twice,

But three times more.

You evade me,

Sweet Home.

Dangling in front,

You tease me.

Only part of you,

Resides in my vessel.

As it shall remain,

You are a feeling.

Nothing more,

Sweet Home.

"The Rights of Pride"

American tribute,

Land of the free.

Prideful sins,

National misery.

Stand loud,

Stand brave.

Bludgeoned death,

Cause of hate.

Take pride,

Stand guard.

"Bill of Wrath"

I succumb to the fury of my beastly instincts.

Red blood floods my eyes.

Shouting viscously,

I crave anger.

Fire and smoke wallop cheeks.

It suffocates.

"In the Depths"

Sinking in the depths,

A light appears.

I shiver in my vessel,

Tentacles show fangs.

My vessel is consumed,

Blackness devours my mind.

The Kraken naps,

With a full belly of thought.

The jellies rejoice,

Their King has eaten.

No sting, all bite.

The depths rejoice,

The King is full.

"Faulty Rhythm"

Trickling Lollipops,

With Vandershnoo Dew.

Wampering Riff Raff,

Fallawampee Biggle Boo.

Slithertingy Fasherta,

Kickley Noodle Wang.

Moontaple Shwee,

Vegetoonies Lickertang.

Alas, the Crimpledots Purpnuttertas.

"Ticking Upon the Bricks"

Walking around the slender hides,

Ticking upon the bricks.

Chirps from the chicks,

Moisten Thy lips.

Belching around the noggin slew,

Plucking upon the rucks.

Stones collide,

Etching is imminent.

Puzzle pipes red hot,

Steamers cool the mass.

"The Quarry"

Platinum picks from the conveyer,

The mineral keeps its value.

Excavate minds,

Note the pit's depth.

Blast out rocky insignificance,

For the gold lay beyond.

Nuggets of truth,

Diamonds press on.

Salvage the wreckage,

Pocket the treasure.

Burrow some more,

Collect the pleasure.

The quarry is open always.

"The Toad & His Princess"

Sitting on his stool,

The mushroom drips.

Princess sleepwalks,

While the Toad flips.

Tripping on her beauty,

Stoned to death.

He croaks to her,

Longing for her.

Princess awakens,

The toad jumps.

He leaps to Princess,

She catches her Prince.

Loving touch,

Warm hearts.

He croaks to her,

Longing for her.

The Princess drips.

"The Addict I Am"

My lungs beg for rest,

As my body burns with tar.

Charred and cracked,

Throat singed from flame.

Pleasure sticks,

Candied glue,

And Caviar powder.

Celebratory snacks,

Daily diets submit.

My mind begs for more,

As my body implodes.

Not for desire,

But necessity.

Addict myself,

To delightful highs.

Substance or not,

The chain tightens around my neck.

Giving up is for losers.

"Transmutational Era of the Future"

It will be strange, no doubt, seeing the future when we arrive there 40 years from now, or 60 years, or further. Good wishes of well being to all, as we travel sluggishly on earth's timescale. Sluggishly for good reason, of course. I wonder what sort of horrifying freakish mutants we will encounter in mankind's evolution. I am a freak remember, a mutant telepath and telekinetic time traveler who moves objects with my mind, floating throughout spacetime, teleporting with my Jeep Liberty Sport. Many people find meditation to be a calming way to repress anxiety and balance their spiritual aura within their seven chakras. I know nothing of these magical spells and mischievous child's play; although, I would certainly recommend the council of high witches and warlocks for future inquiries. Crystal shops and bong stores are more suitable for such noble secrets of the universe and meditation's suggestive practices. I lobby for mutation, not meditation. Rather than empty your mind, expand your comprehension with massive mysteries of our universe. Stretch your thoughts, your dreams, your curiosity, your emotions, your beliefs, and your principles or ethics. Contort your mind's abyss into various unbelievable shapes you were unable to comprehend before practicing mutation. Ponder the most outrageous of thoughts carefully navigating the quarry of your own mind. The future will breed transmutational generations that can manipulate spacetime like we have never seen before. With information so readily available for uploading and downloading, comprehensive minds of the future will create unimaginable structures, extraordinary ships, intelligent transportation, and free energy will be abundant for adoptive users everywhere. Meditation is meaningful; mutation is evolutionary.

"The Burning of a Witch"

A beautiful blasphemer is roped,

Her ankles are worn with rub.

Cursed opinions of pilgrims,

Logs cradle her poor feet.

Shoulders weak,

Her exhaust consumes.

Brunette hair slithers,

Near an emblem on her bosom.

A star of steel,

Inverted for affection.

The witch lifts her head,

A mob of filth roars.

With one last breathe,

Her torch is lit.

She screams to death,

Asking why.

"Mechanical Mastery"

Gears rotate submissively,

An idea generates energy.

Pulleys and ropes synchronize,

Weight is lifted by hour.

The gears turn, Rods rotating.

Clicking and ticking,

Clicking and ticking.

Springs tense in place,

Ready the cannon.

Clicking and ticking.

A snap and lock,

Positions are firm.

Silence is loud,

Ticks and clicks hush.

No ticks.

No clicks.

Release.

"My Hemorrhaging Brain"

It bleeds with profanity,

But heals with candor.

Tis gentle, kind, and careful,

Armed with combative mirrors.

My glands are swollen,

With apologetic anger.

Relieved by the monsoon,

Of moist pleasure.

The stem of my thoughts,

Sourced from a wound.

Submerged in my consciousness,

I bleed onto the floor of possibility.

The pool of my thoughts,

Drains to the stem of my wound.

It empties and filters,

But continues to hemorrhage.

No cloth to bandage,

Such vast laceration.

Nothing to cauterize,

Crippling devastation.

Truth can wound,

More so than a lie.

I will hemorrhage forever,

Until the day I die.

"American Literature"

A novice,

For our country is young.

We arrogantly pride,

We arrogantly state.

United and bound,

Pages are banned.

Writings of will,

Writings of wonder.

Treasonous distaste,

Opinions to ponder.

A novice,

For our country is young.

She is a teenager,

With pimples and zits.

Braces on her teeth,

Forming proper smiles.

In writing we trust,

The opinion of our own.

Freedom is flawed,

Future unknown.

Lead us not,

Into damnation.

We the people,

Trust nothing.

"Jolly Roger & His 40 Keys"

Jingling,

Jangling,

Jinkers,

Jolly fiddles his fingers.

Clinking, Clanking, Clinkers,

None of the keys fit his wife.

"Saturated"

The world is full,

Yet we require more.

Rarity is dimmed,

By celebrity hoard.

Value is cheap,

Markets fatigued.

Fresh is desired,

Shelf life expired.

Cravings of new,

In constant waves of blast.

Absorbed by the glob,

Industries unicorn.

Nourished with currency,

Products materialize.

Matter is nonsense,

Materials are thought.

Marinate the world,

With abrupt sanity.

"Ancient Conquerors & their Missions"

I imagine the conquerors of eons past were absolute psychopaths. They must have been so mad, among their communities, that everyone feared they would be killed if they did not follow orders from their conquering psychopath. This sounds terrifying, living when hoards of men would follow a psychopath into unfamiliar territory only to slaughter people, enslave them, or abuse the community for pleasure and pilfering. I am grateful I live in the 21st Century, where our psychopaths where suits and ties, controlling our country with legislature, bulldozing their path through the American people to their thrown of corruption. Times have changed; people have not. The desire for power is just as great today as it was when ancient civilizations were developing their kingdoms. The desire for power, authority, titles, social status, and the desire to be more than what you were, more than what other people are. What organic thought process was programed to our puny brains instinctively craving these things? What motives enticed the ancient conquerors when planning to commit genocide on entire colonies or tribes? It must have been horrifying, to say the least, to live in these periods of terror and murderous rampage. Why embark on such an arrogant adventure? Why conquer? Why did these figures desire to rule the world? What compelled leaders to expand their territory, and why was there less compromised and more combat? Well, we as humans are incredibly stupid. In fact, we are so stupid, we have no imagination about how stupid we are, hence our tiny comprehensions have only allowed us to evolve to the year 2024, where we prioritize popularity, glamour, huge inventories of stuff, fake tits, inclusive cartoons, and pocket TVs that allow us to watch people lick each other's buttholes. I love this world, let me not fool you, less of the butthole licking, but more of the amazing titties and everything else, that is the ape in me; I am incredibly stoked to be fused together in the extraterrestrial abyss puzzle with all you freaky people. We certainly are a fascinating species, we only need expansion and management to further a more advanced civilization. Back to our Ancient Conquerors: they must have been absolute psychopaths; conquerors are much different than explorers. Conquerors search to destroy, pilfer, rebuild in their image, or move on after their destructive blitzkrieg, maintaining dominance along the damaging path. Explorers search to observe possibilities, questioning why, how, or what if. The comparison between the two titles is linked with the common trait of advancement. The two figures long to search outside of their contained comprehensions, attempting to achieve a goal, or to expand their reign. For the conqueror, their mission is to rule the world; for the explorer, to observe the world.

"The Mission"

Ready your sails,

Scope the course.

Batten the hatch,

Light your torch.

Maps are tattered,

Gunpowder stowed.

Hostiles abound,

Exploring unknown.

Waters are angry,

Waters are fierce.

Ship holds tough,

Storms will clear.

Observe and report,

Captain's log jots.

Pages to ponder,

Conquered the plot.

"Never After"

A golden carriage travels,

Through a spiraling puzzle of madness.

The chariot is slow,

Surround is lightspeed.

Horsed with power and thought,

The engines gallop valiantly.

Firing cylinders of sparkling mystery,

Ignition explodes into oblivion.

On second thought,

We travel like snails on a grassy plain.

Its shell as our chariot,

We arrive never after.

"Aggressive Passing"

Toxicity in a hood,

Cloaked with resent.

Thin ice cracked,

Petty footsteps around.

A dance of disappointment,

In fields of repulsion.

Passing the past,

Emotions are nicked.

Thoughts of crass,

Tension reacts,

Aggressively tricked.

"The Hunger"

Greedy demons,

Thieves of thought.

A virus of violence,

Well-fed or not.

They feast,

They bloat,

They feast some more.

A carnival of games,

Admission is free.

You are the prize,

When hunger feeds.

Fasting is futile,

Diets are core.

Desire cannot wait,

It is hungry for more.

"The Psychedelic Experience"

An individual need not ingest substance to experience psychedelic wonder; however, they do allow expansion of thought and incredible imaginative slideshows, I must admit. Since our universe is constructed of God's thoughts, one could argue that the imaginative slideshows are less imaginary and paint an ethereal version of our questionable reality. Why do these psychedelics exist? What curiosities were they satisfying when explorers came across such thought-provoking substances? If you have ever ingested psychedelic substances before reading this, what curiosities, in your own mind, were you attempting to satisfy? Every day, psychedelic wonder is abundant instantly upon opening your eyes. Everything in your sight is magic, mystery, and wonder. No universal matter, dark or grey, exists that was not previously fused into the abyss puzzle extraterrestrial that once was intact before thinking our universe into existence. A psychedelic experience can be interpreted in an infinite number of ways, but the typical daily thoughts of our 8 billion brothers and sisters would be considered psychedelic enough for my own puny human brain. Life and thought are equally psychedelic, and our experience here on earth, in our human forms, should be taken not lightly, but as heavy as the gravity bound inside our atmosphere. A psychedelic experience is food for thought, a snack for the brain to gnaw. Epiphanies are psychedelic as they are breakthroughs in your own comprehension; however, you need not take illicit substance to spawn epiphanies, only immense thought provocation. The individual should thoroughly research their own comprehension, their own state of mind, their own wellbeing, previously to embarking on a psychedelic journey using substance, but I am suggesting you can travel there without ingesting anything. You can travel on a psychedelic journey in your mind, sitting content with your imagination's infinite courses. I advise no one in this world; I report only my psychedelic experiences.

"Eternal Flower"

Flowing across sidewalks,

Tripping on thought.

A powerful sprout,

Peaks its pedals.

Ultraviolet stem,

Colorful array.

Each second passes,

New spectrums display.

Tranced by beauty,

I stare as a dunce.

Perennial stages,

Prism of light.

Eternally blooming,

Blossoming bright.

"A Bag of Jellybeans"

My jellies are jelly,

Globbing good goos.

I offer a bean,

Besting the bunch.

The dripping of jellies,

Jams the drizzle.

My bag is goopy,

And gooding with glop.

Jellies are jazzing,

Gooping a lot.

Picking the jellies,

That gel in the just.

Jelly my beans,

Baggage a must.

"Church of Behavior"

I choose not to attend any service, for I practice good behavior and kind thought towards others. My church service is daily, giving thanks to the Almighty, praising him for all of existence, graciously requesting his guidance and forgiveness. No denomination can bind my mind that God himself provided me upon birth. This world is extremely difficult for all who walk on his blue earth regardless of class, status, or worth. If his son, Jesus, our brother from the holy mother, were to be present in our 21st century, traveling through time alongside his followers, I imagine he would be a trillionaire with his ability to turn water to wine. Jesus Christ, what an incredible ability to possess, his comprehension was obviously extreme and distant beyond our own. Peace be with everyone, as we travel through time and space together, as one with the universe. Let us share sips from the Almighty chalice of sex and rock'n'roll; do not spill the goblet of peace and love, for the Almighty juices will eternally flow away from his intended existence. We slurp from the goblet feverishly and forever. Our church has no walls, no podium, no pews, no stage, no emblems, no barriers of comprehension; however, God is observing our behavior, no doubt. Amen.

"Our Skeletal Strings"

Pinching and pulling,

Cracking and snapping,

The marrow is full of life.

Fraying and tearing,

Ripping and stretching,

Tensions cut with a knife.

Guiding our vessel,

Along the earth trestle,

Pulled by attraction in sight.

Bound to the ground,

Gravity is found,

If not, we would all take flight.

The strings they sing,

In harmonious fling,

Unless they are wound too tight.

Our bones are brittle,

But played like a fiddle,

At rest is when they delight.

"Worthless Monk"

The worthless monk delivers concise information about the universe, yet only contributes to their own version of realistic satisfaction and dictation. Their function is to ponder our existence with lack of precision, balancing thought with non-judgmental guidance. I admire a monk's ability to harness their chi, and deliver prolific advice to a world they conceal themselves in. I have no judgements against monks, they are peaceful people and the title of worthless was not intended to appropriate a condescending slander of their existence; the only intention is to intrigue minds with new methods of thinking and encourage the expansion of their thoughts. Monks serve great purpose in our world, and their existence is imperative to our universal healing process. A monk must conceal themselves inside their own version of realistic satisfaction and dictation because of our inherent worthlessness in a world dominated by hatred and disgust for one another, hence the requirement for their own monasteries with borders to protect their peace, their chakras, their chi, their souls, and wellbeing. In this world, when an individual speaks freely about their thoughts, they experience an immediate response from society and the mafia of malicious media frenzy. The monk is worth most to themselves, others interpret the monk's existence as an option for their own, then the non-monkish folk select how to realistically satisfy and dictate their own existence. I am a worthless monk who is an apish addict of mystery and wonder with no advice or guidance to deliver, only gelatinous goo in the form of bound pages riddled with poetry and pondering.

"A Product of Our Environment"

The soil in which a plant grows is a significant factor in the health and prosperity of its production. Healthy soil, proper pruning, sufficient watering, all will contribute to a vigorous life-cycle that boasts bountiful beauty in a nourishing environment. A seed that sprouts in ailing soil infected with unhealthy decay and anti-nutrients, without proper pruning or sufficient watering, the plant will mold and rot from fungal fury in an unforgiving and contaminated environment. Thoughts, behavior, words, activities, materials, consumption, are all variables in an individual's environment, and as you travel through time across our planetary dimension, you will always be instinctively adapting to the physical environment you live within, often against your will. As humans, we have the free will to change our environments, moving freely across the country, or continent, from town to town, state to state, across international borders to settle down in a new country to call home. We can decorate our homes as we wish, we can choose what genre of music we listen to, we can decide what movies we enjoy watching, all of which is creating an adaptation of yourself within your designated environment. The individuals you surround yourself with possess the biggest influence over you; the individuals surrounded by yourself will be influenced by your possession. Becoming a product of our environment is inescapable and serves as a binding contract signed in personality and behavior on the parchment of society.

"To Mock is to Mend"

Above all,

Joke in the dark.

Protect yourself,

With satirical spark.

Mocking is to care,

As mending is to heal.

Judge me not,

For comedic relief.

Judge me not,

For conspiring belief.

We sillied with Sally,

Laughed in a rally,

And forgot the reason of wrong.

Above all,

Joke in the dark.

"The Ballad of a Boogerface"

The nasty slosh of mucus runnith down Thy face.

Snotty notes of vomit inducing visuals grace our presence.

A symphony of sneezes and tumultuous tissue papers.

The boogerface blunders their nostrils.

A dance of the neck and chin,

Running under Thy fingered palms clasping a cloth.

An immunity instinct to rid out rhinos.

Beware of a rogue Ah-choo.

"Snooty McDoogins"

Snooty sniffled swiftly,

Snickering soft and sound.

The McDoogins doogled the doggle,

Diggling Dagger's dessert.

Snooty snausaged the snoozer,

Slipping slumberly in McDooginville.

"The Dumbest Mother Fucker on the Planet"

The dumbest mother fucker on the planet is smart, they slip through life's fingertips as they relish the freedom of ignorance and the satisfaction of not knowing, not caring enough to know, or acting like they do not know. The dumbest mother fucker on the planet is slime in the palm of society, adapting and morphing with each finger's manipulative gesture or malicious poke. The DMF is resilient to the perpetual molding of civilization and will live eternally in the cosmos of our universe. An argument could be made that achieving the status of DMF is complete bliss within the realm of our planetary reality; however, the title is less appealing than the comprehension of its underlying implication. Suggesting the dumbest mother fucker on the planet is ironically intelligent could be interpreted as an elaborate expansion of the phrase Ignorance is Bliss; the well-known phrase has less suggestive meaning than my analysis of the dumbest mother fucker on the planet. I am proposing the expression, Ignorance is Bliss, lacks a certain implication of intelligent ignorance, the ability to act, or play dumb. I lobby for the modification of the saying to read as Acting Is Bliss, therefore I am the dumbest mother fucker on the planet, and I know nothing of anything, apart from goo.

"American Racket"

Terrorizing friendlies,

Fire over our heads.

Manipulative media,

Neutralized or dead.

Sound the alarm,

No one has ears.

Sweeping the threat,

With self-induced fears.

Rack up the pity,

Rack up the joy.

Rack up the city,

Rack up their toys.

Barreling through,

Chest out for moxie.

Minds gone askew,

From an American proxy.

"Deserving"

When an individual is questioned why they deserve something desirable, the circumstances of one's life are often verbalized in the pitch of their own explanation of why they think they deserve something. The pitched justification is typically armored with misfortunes or unrelated circumstances that are conveniently positioned in the doorway to deserving the desirable. I am certainly guilty of pitching justifications with the use of misfortunes and explanations of excuses rather than owning and accepting current circumstances, working through whatever obstacles positioned in my route to the doorway of deserving. The question to ask yourself, before justifying your merit, is what am I doing to deserve this, not, what happened to me? This is difficult to push aside devastation, heartbreak, and loss, when rationalizing merit for deserving the desirable; perhaps, the misfortunes could be explained in a more lesson-learning manner compared to a venting therapy session. "I deserve this because I learned, and experienced, many different methods of practicing a particular (or multiple) field(s) of study (or trades) and have applied my knowledge from both my successes and failures on my journey to deserving the desirable." A practical statement for verbalizing merit in a world that has no regard for you or your unfortunate circumstances. This statement can be adapted, or molded, as needed for any reader's own life's journey; instead of, "I deserve this," it should read, "I deserve your business," and instead of, "deserving the desirable," replace this with, "achieving my personal goals." Again, mold and shapeshift as needed, I advise no one. A devilish spanking by a bohemian goddess is what I surely deserve.

"Digression of a Don"

Distracted by many,

All who come to play.

Little is too much,

And much too little.

Back on topic,

Order in session.

Gavel the court,

Enough with digression.

"May I Have Your Attention Please"

Come one,

Come all,

Seat the front row.

Tent full,

Tent tall,

Enjoy the freak show.

Murmuring and clamoring,

Chittering and chattering,

The show is about to begin.

"A Ninja and the Sword"

Robed with night's darkness,

Steps hover in silence.

Evil threats of malice,

The warrior sprints to battle.

Elemental surprise,

A sword is unsheathed.

The blade cuts deep,

Seppuku.

"The Man Maid"

A butlerish husband,

With skill in the trade.

Plumbing and cleaning,

No need for a maid.

Home to hold on,

Home to relax.

Ready the dinner,

When family gets back.

Burn up the stove,

Heat down the halls.

Lock up the bathroom,

When nature calls.

Chop up the drama,

Chop down the beef.

Veggies on the couch,

After everyone eats.

Dessert for the lot,

Dessert for the Queen.

Scooped in a bowl,

I forgot to feed the dogs.

"Lame"

Tis not the time to do,

Tis the time to not.

Not the time to tis,

Do time tis not the to.

"Marvelous Mischief"

Scurry to the shadows,

Solitude in droves.

Personal touch of pinch,

Playful flames of seduction.

Careful not to burn,

With a slip of your induction.

"Sexual Innuendos"

A stiff arrival,

Hard from handling.

Nippy air,

Points toward pleasure.

Finger foods,

Moistens the meat.

A back door delivery,

Receptacle plugged.

Around the rim we go,

Tongue and cheeky.

Blow my head off,

Explosive load.

Backseat missionary,

Doggy on the couch.

Cream of the crop,

Come together.

Morning mahogany,

Breakfast in bed.

Sausage and eggs,

Keep her well-fed.

"White Rabbit, White Rabbit"

Smokey eyes blur sight,

Fires of idea and thought.

When the smoke clears,

A rabbit hole appears,

Down it I go, why not?

White Rabbit, White Rabbit,

Clear Thy smoke from I.

White Rabbit, White Rabbit,

Show me the vision of my.

Down I go,

In a tunnel of know,

Chasing my tail from behind.

White Rabbit, White Rabbit,

Clear Thy smoke from I.

"The Magician & His Hat"

In my hat,

Lives a factory.

This factory, Makes toys.

The toys are for you,

And you are for I.

The factory is run by rabbits,

Who smoke while they work.

Their boss is a bunny,

Exercising their wheel.

For my next trick,

I will make you a deal.

"Zero Cell Energy"

We, as humans, have the ability to create a more prosperous future for ourselves, our children, grandchildren, great-grandchildren, and so on; our contained comprehensions, our worries, our risk aversion process in our brains, all slow us down in real time and prevent progression or expansion of our comprehensive strength. Perhaps, beginning this book of poetry, theory, pondering, and goo, you will have expanded slightly your own comprehension by questioning literary arithmetic, our universal existence, or the fabrics of time and space. In 2024, humanity can facilitate free energy on a global scale, but we are contained within the multi-trillion-dollar power industries' comprehension. These electric companies could, hypothetically, invest in new innovative technologies to create an infinite grid of energy that is produced by a national transportation system. What are these modern technologies? How could this be free? Power companies, and their billions of dollars, can also invest in other secure assets that provide a healthy outlook for the future, like transportation and the trillions of dollars to be profited after creating a free energy system for America. These companies can create such a system by use of electromagnetic induction, creating cylindrical subway systems constructed of pyrolytic carbon, a light-weight diamagnetic material, carrying railcars fashioned with magnetic surfaces. The magnetic railcars would virtually float inside the cylindrical pyrolytic carbon tube due to the repulsive magnetic field against the cylindrical graphite. The carbon subway cylinder could then be wrapped in copper coils, and during a magnetic railcar commute through the subway, it creates an electromagnetic induction powering itself, towns, counties, states, our entire country, then the entire world can be provided with sustainable, free energy, created by our will to travel places, our necessity to ship materials, our passions for the world and connecting with new possibilities. The electromagnetic train would essentially be a battery for itself and whatever we choose to operate using its produced energy. Imagine a shake-light flashlight, and the concept of shaking the flashlight vigorously five or six times then turning the flashlight on. As the flashlight shakes, a magnet passes through a copper coil within the handle of the flashlight, thus creating an electromagnetic induction. Think of the flashlight's magnet as a railcar transporting passengers, or freight, and think of the flashlight handle as the subway cylinder. Continuous commuting from different stations would produce an electromagnetic induction powerful enough to fuel our country's energy grid. No combustible engine would be required for such a vehicle floating in zero gravity, the railcar's controls would consist of gears and levers manipulating magnetic plates to repel or attract as needed for each specific route of travel. The zero emissions, zero gravity appeal to a free energy future sounds too good to be true; well, for now it shall remain that way until more collaborative efforts are made from behemoth companies controlling different aspects of our lives. Imagine a power producing train that you can ride anywhere around your city, or to the next city, or the next state. Purchasing a transport ticket would be justified knowing your contribution to travel expenses provides a free energy society in which you chose to be part of. The hypothetical pyrolytic carbon subway could alternatively be constructed of a thick copper conductor, while keeping the railcars magnetic, either floating, or fastened to a conventional track. Flying cars was achievable nearly a century ago; we chose a different route with combustible engines and the requirement for oil, fuel, and masculine amounts of horsepower. The helicopter, the plane, blimps, and other aerospace crafts are all real-world examples of flying cars in the modern world. We humans imagined something different with flying cars based on imaginative books and Hollywood movies with their endless variety of versions for our future of humankind. The flying car future, we humans imagine, is a more synchronized floating grid of motor vehicles that teleports our bags of bones to and from our desired destinations. The problem with a floating grid of flying motor vehicles is containment. We can easily make vehicles float by use of magnetic energy; the equation's difficulty lies in stabilizing your vehicle and keeping it stationed on the grid, a specific height above the ground or platform without flying off into oblivion. Our hypothetical subway cylinder contains potential vehicles, or railcars, inside the tube of either pyrolytic carbon or copper conductor, thus providing a safe environment for the flying cars to float from one departure point to

129

their desired destination using manipulated magnetic attraction and repulsion. Had we chosen this direction a century ago, our comprehensive strength for a more movie-like flying vehicular grid would have more than likely been our modern transportation system in the early 21st century. We chose cars that can blow up, crash at immense speeds, tragically kill daily, cars that cost a fortune, both to purchase and to maintain; that is what we as humans chose for mankind. Again, I love this world, and all the amazing stuff; let us expand on our current infrastructure, knowledge, and desires, to further our global unity constructing a better tomorrow. Let me elaborate further on the Zero Cell Energy plan. The subway transportation system would not require a cylindrical shape, but could be fashioned into a square, or elongated rectangular sleeve, to accommodate several service routes transporting patrons inside a brigade of magnetic railcars all while producing its own power. Why haven't we done this already? Well, to build such a transportation system, it would cost our country hundreds of billions of dollars, if not more, and it would also require decades of research, testing, and engineering to construct the safest transportation system in America that floats underneath our cities using Zero Cell Energy. Zero emissions, zero gravity, zero combustion, a subway system using magnetic fields and copper conductors would create the safest, and coolest, way to travel since the commercialization of air travel. What are some foreseen problems in our journey to a flying car subway system using magnetic energy? I think of pacemakers, jewelry, metal rods from surgery, anything that would be a potential hazard inside a magnetic field. Eliminating the possibility of death or injury with surgical metal, pacemakers, or any magnetic metals traveling patrons may have on their persons during transport, is the most significant burden in a transportation system like the Zero Cell Energy proposal. The theoretical energy producing transport system, applicable to other suitable platforms, could power hotels, skyscrapers, any building with an elevator shaft. The elevator can be retrofitted with a copper conductor sleeve, the elevator car can be fashioned with magnetic surfaces inducing the electromagnetic current when the elevator is in operation. A magnetic elevator transporting patrons, or guests, from

130

floor to floor, while producing power for the entire building. Oh yes, the elevator would be floating, I forgot to mention. A floating, non-cabled elevator system that produces energy for an entire city block. If I am killed before the publication of this book, the reasonable cause may be for this Zero Cell Energy plan of mine; I mean our plan. I know those filthy grease balls making billions in the auto industry and the power industry would love to rip me apart and bury this idea as if it were never written. Ha! The nincompoop numbskulls will never take me alive! Phooey on them and their greedy ways of insufferable oppression. The unity of minds will create a fantastic future of freedom when the barriers of comprehension are broken and explode into a universe of underground floating cars. Why would we not have flying cars, and why would we not put them underground? Let us step into the future, or float if you will. Can we all agree, floating cars are flying cars?

"Practical vs. Possible"

Slowing ourselves down with our practical logic and risk aversion processes, we tend to avoid thinking outside of the hypothetical box we all create for ourselves. Possibilities are commonly obscured beyond a barrier of measurable comprehension inside an individual's mind preventing them from seeing beyond a certain perspective. In most cases, our world is bound within a certain capacity of comprehension due to the practicalities of how our world is governed, and what is considered logical, or convenient, or technically impossible under current circumstances. Our evolutionary trajectory is dependent on breaking the barrier of practicality into the dimension of what is possible. It is the practical thinker that halts our future in time; the person who thinks in terms of possibilities paints the measurable canvas of time using creation's fine bristled brush. The possible can become practical over time and space, for they are both physical magnets of concept with two opposite poles equally equipped with attractive and repulsive ends. We only need to adjust the poles, slightly correcting the attraction of concepts, connecting our puzzle pieces in the appropriate manner.

"Sticks & Stones"

They are but words,

Which can beat and belittle.

Verbally torturous,

Phrases that cripple.

Blunt and rigid,

Tough and rough.

Similes and metaphors,

Struck in the head,

Like a slap in the face.

Tools of the tongue,

Sheen of your teeth,

Intentionally lacks taste.

Sticks and stones,

Nor rocks and logs,

Will cower me loud.

Understand thee well,

Your plot of grin and sin.

Understand thee well,

Your powerful wordy spin.

"An Educated Guess"

My literary publications go unaccredited stamped with no certificates, plaques, or degrees, for this is my very first publication of stoney sophistication. I have much experience in the real world of our modern American society and have sat atop fortune's mountain as well as slept in the gutter of broke boulevard. My thoughts, ideas, and theories are all organically generated from my observing mind which carefully gathers notes from the active surrounding world. What is fortune to you? My educated guess states the claim we humans can bend, mold, and break this concept of fortune since other concepts like comprehension, practicality, and time can all be bent, stretched, folded, or even broken. The concept of fortune is collectively imagined as a monetary amount large enough to become free from outside influence or control. The amount will vary depending on the individual's perception of what sum of money is considered a fortune, or their perception of how much money is required to live free outside of influence and control. Monetary fortune is only a singular concept within the borders of perceived fortune. Some could argue that a monetary fortune is required to receive proper schooling which would provide proper degrees and certifications to secure more prosperous careers in their post-college lives. The word fortunate should be carefully examined and investigated, fitting where your life is satisfying. We, the people, tend to see more of what we do not have rather than see what we already possess. With so many sources of information and knowledge in our 21st century, why would an individual not learn what they wish studying books, videos, or social media influencer tips? I have no college degree, no accredited document other than a high school diploma, yet I have formed educated guesses on all of existence and am satisfied knowing our human comprehensive strength is too weak to fully understand what our function of existence is, or the precise dynamics of our universe. In the year 2024, our human civilization has only scientific data explaining how our universe is, not why our universe is. Why are we here? Why do we exist? Why is the universe so expansive and yet we are only now learning about our abilities to travel through space and time? I answer these existential questions with only educated guesses based on collective data, experience, and knowledge, from the world of which we created our reality. Our answers to the how's and why's can only be formulated with collected evidence our human race has cooperatively agreed to understand in a certain form of scientific context. Earth's population includes so many brilliant minds, free with thought, experts in their scientific fields, or trades, or whatever; although our earthly population is filled with brilliant geniuses, we still have no answers beyond theory and speculation for our entire existence, only an educated guess.

"Dark Brilliance"

Utterly tragic,

Knowing impossible is possible.

Universal magic,

Brilliance held responsible.

Darkness to beauty,

Decay to blush.

Slowed from light,

Glowing folk with fear.

Wizards of the world,

Spells choired unclear.

Intelligence and ignorance,

A repelling force of nature.

Brilliance held responsible,

In the darkness of danger.

"The Existential Equation"

$$\text{Existence} = \frac{(\text{Time} + \text{Comprehension})}{\text{All Universal Matter}} \quad (\text{The Unknown})$$

The proposed equation, which unlocks the answer to our very existence, is only theoretical, and even in theory this equation would never be solved due to the unknown variable powering the numerator of the existential math problem. We do not know what we do not know, and will only come to understand, or comprehend, newfound knowledge when our comprehensive thoughts expand beyond their current barriers. Uncovering clues to our existence is heavily dependent on our expanding comprehension and exploring the unknown. To put this into different context, or perspective, our human-caused reality is so extremely far from our actual existential reality, it would literally blow-up our minds if put into physical perspective our universe compared to our human size. I imagine our nervous system would completely shut down with massive overload from thought-processing causing either an immediate death, or a more violent convulsive epileptic seizure leading to an inevitable death by broken comprehension. We are so unbelievably tiny we have no idea how small humans, in point of fact, measure in the scale of our universe, and to fathom an entity larger than our entire observable universe thinking all matter into existence is one the most comprehension-bending concepts I can personally think of and articulate in the form of text. Another concept devised from this equation suggests that our existence is what we comprehend it to be over our lifetimes, or the collective universal lifetime. In summation, our existence may never truly be comprehensible, the identifiable space of the unknown will never be completely uncovered, for there will always be mysteries beyond our comprehensive barriers, but also extraordinary new subjects to intrigue curiosity. For all you science majors, and salty sophisticated people, below is a different example of the same equation using symbols and units.

"Serpents in the Shallows"

I am a frozen fish stick,

Treading above water.

My gills absorb data,

Filtering functionality.

I breathe liquid wonder,

And breed a school of asking.

My ocean home is dark,

Filled with monsters of the depths,

But also, serpents in the shallows.

"A Crystal-Clear Idea"

It is the world,

And her madness.

The hatred,

The sadness.

Clarity of concept,

Crystalizes from time.

Changing a threat,

To loving protect.

A bulb that's caring,

Shining freedom.

Inception of dreams,

Too bright to see them.

Blinded,

Scarred,

And disabled.

An energy that differs,

Deserves a new table.

Pulsing power,

Stored in memory.

Visions of reality,

Clashes actuality.

"Pipping the Pipes with Polly"

I pipped till Polly pepped,

Pipping Polly's pipes periodically.

Popping pipes Polly preferred,

But pipping is Polly's present.

Polly's pipes pipped,

And they pupped.

The pupping of Polly's pipes,

Popped the pepping,

And Polly pipped pipes with I.

"Forgotten Time"

No backpedaling,

Only in the mind.

No ticking in the past,

To forgotten time.

Why do we wish,

Why do we want?

Traveling back,

Avoid ghostly haunt.

No need to worry,

No need to fright.

Time on our side,

Travel in dream tonight.

"Fashionably Late"

Red carpets,

Doors fling.

Silence bursts,

Grinning scene.

Gawky crowd,

Laser my eyes.

Party resume,

Thee toast of mine.

"Worship & Sacrifice"

I am nothing,

Blessed with existence.

Worshiping everything,

Sight grants into vision.

Faith to almighty,

Faith to Thy own.

Studious lectures,

On a sacrificial throne.

I am nothing,

Blessed with existence.

My sacrifice is to be,

Never to become,

As yours to be you.

"Salty Sophistication"

Caviar chandeliers,

With pinkish blue roses.

Golden handrails,

With marmalade hoses.

Monocle for focus,

Armored with a cane.

Hat for status,

Coat for the same.

Pass me a dime sir,

Pass me a nickel.

Surely, you will receive,

A karmic gold riddle.

Pass me a quarter sir,

Pass me a bill.

Lay down your cane sir,

Profit you will.

"Canceling Crowd"

Voicing fury,

Green eyes.

Up in a hurry,

Down to size.

Fan or foe,

Understood or not.

The crowd cries.

"The Tools of Writ"

Order the chaos,

Flicking wrist with reason.

Who signs?

Who writes?

Who thinks?

All may read,

All may not bear.

A controlling hand,

In text and torment.

Demanding rule,

Protection dormant.

A box of tools,

Variety of power.

Lest the people,

Give up their cower.

"The 100-Year Idea"

Plant yesterday,

Water today,

Water tomorrow.

Harvest nothing,

Prune as needed.

"Subatomic"

Within the nuclei,

Strings dance upon lumps.

Hurricanes of forces,

Construct annihilation.

It is cold here,

No air to breathe.

I see no "sky," I see no "clouds,"

Only storms of forces.

Lightning is gassy,

Thunderclaps in blocky waves.

A kaleidoscopic scene,

Consciously rotating in fury;

Although, nothing is aware,

All is celestial.

It rains embers here.

Freezing into obliteration,

Before colliding with another.

A colorful festive fire ball.

Bullets revolve angrily,

With brutish belligerence.

"Dead Man Walking"

Embalmed with knowledge of death,

I am aging dust collecting memories.

Walking a tightrope lit on fire,

Ending for my dusty bones,

Never for my soul's desire.

Jogging your thoughts in twists,

Particulate quantum quips.

When I, and the present, is past,

The walk continues with you.

"The Strangeness of Love"

Hearts and minds,

Pumping red lips.

Chemical reaction,

Electric fingertips.

First sight or not,

Zoned in time.

Nomadic partners,

Away or side-by-side.

Spontaneous combustion,

Crazy with force.

What would you do,

For a lover's remorse?

Strange spells cast,

Triangular attraction.

Heart drips hot,

Brain drips cold.

Eyes crushed to diamonds,

Vision melts to gold.

Souls on the search,

Look with their mind;

Spirits in harmony,

Will connect on time.

"A Gangster in Nerd's Clothing"

The tape between Thine eyes shields bullets.

Thy chest-shield protects thee from more than mere pocket damage,

It shields me from a drive-by dissing and dashing. Ha!

I shoot laser beams from Thine key's ring,

And blast my way through the twerking wenches of Mor.

My racket is scientific,

Calculated with precise lullaby. Ha!

I fly an armored tank of annoyance,

And whitey tighties. Ha!

I challenge thee to a duel!

Allow Thyself to untie Thine shoes from one another,

The duel shall commence immediately thereafter.

Ha! You fool!

I've blasted your head clean off!

Holster my laser, Tip of the cap.

No duels thee lost,

Without Thine rabbit and hat.

"Chompy Goodness"

Chimpy chomped and chewed,

Chewing chompy chunks in church.

Chimpy's church chunked,

Chomping chewing and chimping.

Chimpy chonked,

Chimpy chunked,

And Chimpy churched.

Chimpy is a naughty monkey,

Eating his yummy bananas.

"Burning Wick"

Lit end-to-end,

With anticipation.

It's gone to ash,

As time itself.

"A Cat Named Curiosity"

This cat is cool,

He cruises coinciding with chaos.

A cool cat with crafty questions,

Caring to create conversations.

A colorful cool cat,

Clothed in queries cotton.

Contradicting concerns of kittens,

Curiosity kills cats without a clue,

And coddles kitties with questions.

"Positively Negative"

Yes,

I don't think so.

For sure,

I'm not going.

I can't believe it,

Congratulations!

"The Devil, His Smile & the Trident"

Viscously grim,

Red like rusty roses.

Smirking in sin,

Tempting pokey noses.

Bright eyes of terror,

Sparking in the mirror.

Fallen with a purpose,

Taunting with his trident.

Hellish spikes in threes:

Pressing,

Prodding,

Penetrating.

"The Last Donut"

Don't touch,

My fucking donut.

Sprinkled or glazed,

Just don't.

"Kids Raising Kids"

My kid has a child for a father,

His friends are much the same.

My step-kids are tiny adults,

With parents childish as they.

Kid to kid,

Child to parent,

Managing minis,

Tough I swear it.

My kid has a child for a mother,

His friends are much the same.

Her step-kids are tiny adults,

With parents childish as they.

Kid to kid,

Parent to child,

Organizing offspring,

Raised in the wild.

"A Fetish for Funky Fresh Fluff & Fun"

Slap me with silly,

Bind me with jester.

Choke me with chuckles,

Gag me for pleasure.

Spank me with humor,

Relieve me with tears.

Sit on my face,

For 500 years.

"The Writer"

Playing with a ball of yarn,

Like a retarded kitten with ADHD.

Tip-tapping, Tip-tapping.

Pawing the stringy toy,

Unwinding with each furry punch.

Pushing it away,

Only to sprint forward.

Tip-tapping, Tip-tapping.

Pawing and playing again.

"The Pimp & His Hoes"

Tis a sublime and subtle feeling of security,

A pimp slapping his hoes.

Leopard purses hiding bruised knees,

Hoeish divinity as everyone knows.

Feminine entrepreneurs,

With a managing hand.

Big Daddy boss with a coat,

Slappy happy controlling his remote.

Pimping is business,

Pimping is life.

The pimp and his hoes,

Deserves a rewrite.

"Tinted Glass"

Rollin up,

Shade thrown.

See-through,

Driving slow.

Crack the glass,

Hot box vent.

Suited hand,

Heavy scent.

Foes clapped,

Hit the seat.

Glasses tint,

Foggy heat.

"Milk & Cookies"

Submerged in dairy fluid,

I slowly disintegrate.

Chunky and moist,

Tis a palatable date.

Crumbles of my dough,

Form a muddy-moo pie.

Clinch the beaker,

No sips could dry.

Sip and chew,

Then sip some more.

My chips fall off,

They drop to the floor.

"Chemistry"

Experimental relations,

Transformative creations.

Magic and blasphemy,

Concoctive recipes.

Stirring and sifting,

Bubbling and burning.

Molecular bondage,

Combinations turning.

A mixture of elements,

Periodically tabled.

Coated Lab Knights,

Willingly able.

The sum of all,

Is everything.

"Modern-Day Wizards, Warlocks & Witches"

In the year 2024, our schools of wizardry and witchcraft are defined by perception; this leads to an unknown number of magical mutants that are floating through society unrecognized for their enchantment and evolved freakishness. Most of us humans see a wizard or witch when we are feeling ill, need a prescription, or in case of emergency. Our modern-day doctors could be considered the witches, warlocks, and wizards of ancient times due to their ability to heal, diagnose, and theorize. We also watch wizards, and warlocks, perform heinous acts of blasphemy each time we turn on our television. The television is an evil form of satanic ritualistic sacrifice as the user bows to its power of magical images of illusory manipulation. A pilgrimage of early America would surely burn anyone alive who possessed such devilish devices after slandering them as a witch and tormenting them with a psychological racking. This is only a single, and small example of America's violent history leading us to now, still hating each other for the smallest of reasons. In 2024, we no longer burn people alive; the accused is only flayed alive on national television with immediate response from America and her people, the people whom which have only an evil satanic screen to gather their information, manipulated by the media.

Imagine living 600 years ago, in a small mountain village, playing with some rocks you found. You discovered the magnetic repulsive and attractive poles in two separate units. You are amazed! The pieces effortlessly pinch one another as you move them closer with your hands. You peel them apart, flip them around, then attempt to force the two repulsive ends together feeling the force of magnetism in between. It is magic! You are excited to bring your discovery back to your village's leader and introduce its wonder to your people. You hurry back to the village, your leader is readily accessible near the watering hole, and you run to their side. You pull out your magnetic rocks of magic and display their enchanting abilities of attraction and repulsion.

169

Your leader immediately hits you over the head with his club, ropes your arms and legs, then burns you alive. As your bloody body lay there from the bludgeoned strike, prior to your burning, your leader picks up the magnets and keeps the rocks for themselves playfully smiling at the newfound magical toy.

"My Pet Duck Who Is Ugly"

This thing is fucking grotesque.

It pisses and shits everywhere.

I kick it outside, but it quacks at me.

Fuck this thing.

"Origami"

Fold me,

Shape me.

Spin me,

Flip me.

Just don't,

Tear me.

That's what,

She said.

"Tireless Nights of Extreme Terror"

Awake in a dream,

We play all night.

Thinking about what is,

What could be,

And what should not.

Quickly diverting,

Positive energy to the stop.

Stars guide us in thought;

We are pilots of our own.

Cipher the systems,

And system the cipher.

Now get some sleep.

"The Fisherman & His Holes"

The man enjoyed many,

Three of which his favor.

This landscape was barren,

With clear route to each.

One was peculiar,

Forbidden some say.

Fishermen tell tales,

To this very day.

Fancied his luck,

Casting like a stud.

All he pulled out,

Was a stick in the mud.

"The Cheater"

Eyes in the back of my skull,

I see you cocksucker.

I'll destroy you after class,

And tell your mom.

"Vigilante Justice"

Thumbtacks and ornaments,

Listerine jet fuel.

Hot plate handshake,

Underground fan duel.

Castle in the kitchen,

Gates of steel transparency.

Caped with vengeance,

Billions of dollars sure do help.

"My recent DM from God"

Dear Patience,

Thou art virtue, and a trusted son of thee, who shall behold greatness
in all its glory amongst Thy human creations. Thou art value, care, and
comfort. Thou art sensitive, as are all children of thee; under Thine
divine guidance you shall deliver to the world a new kind of relief and
comfort, a new form of political practice among your species.
Patience, thou art marvelous mystery placed into an infinite jig-saw-
puzzle constructed and framed by thee. Thoughts were heard amongst
the global population. Thy precious time will unfold into a mystery
with thou fingers turning shoulders to gold, and minds to mush. Thou
art a child of thee, and shoulders will certainly turn to gold by taps of
thou fingertips. Beware of the serpents in the shallows and the demons
in the depths; thou art safe with thee, for the blessing of Thy children's
existence will cycle infinitely along the circumcision, I mean
circumference of Thy universe. Thou art all the same, Patience, in
different bodies, with different minds, thinking collectively to carry
out Thy divine purpose. Be good to each other, Thy will be done.

Continue to love,

G

P.S. Of course it was me you fucking idiot, Jesus Christ.

"Nervous Nelly & Her Neat Knots"

Nelly knotted nervously,

Knotting the neat,

And not the knot.

Her need to knot,

Was neat, but nervous.

Nelly's neat knots,

Nervously knocked.

Knocking neat knots,

Nelly knotted nervously.

No knots,

Too neat,

For Nelly.

Now,

She's on,

To knobs.

"Holy Trinity"

We are God's erection,

Per his last email.

Inundated with a big bang,

Theories only trail.

Hail Mary,

Hail Derrick,

Hail Katie,

Hail Mark,

Hail Ceasar's salad full of Grace.

Take a crouton of Thy holy son.

Eat his flesh,

But hold your nose.

Human meat is disgusting,

And tastes nothing of steak.

Drink his blood,

Fucking chug that shit!

Wipe Thy lip with cloth of I,

Deliver us from sin,

And Karen.

Fuck that bitch.

To the Father,

The Son,

And the big bang orgy in the sky.

Amen.

"Don't Laugh"

At a public execution,

Or a song in church.

At grandma's mole,

Or something that hurts.

At someone's misfortune,

Or fabulous flaws.

At sensitive matters,

That drops people's jaws.

At wifey in pain,

Or her princess behavior.

At the in-law's taste,

Or their lack of flavor.

At crowds of prideful clowns,

Or masks of paint and rubber.

At the suits they may wear,

To keep them undercover.

"When a Woman Farts"

Run for the hills,

When the wind blows rough.

Musky death below,

Not reading her bluff.

Get yourself together,

Straighten out your face.

Silent but deadly,

Flatulent fraud case.

Murder by toot,

She fizzled with gas.

A musical note,

From her giggling ass.

"Humor in 2024"

Our society evolved to fatally criticize, or cancel, anything and anyone that is splashed with slander on the national media mob's many channels of manipulation with little to no investigation of thought. In our new sensitive society, a humorous comment meant to provoke laughter and smiles is often interpreted as demeaning, hateful, or offensive. The words one chooses when interacting with anyone should be considered carefully before blurting out unorganized sentences or impulsive junctions to others' statements. Due to our newfound, universal connectivity our senses are heightened with a more powerful interpretive ability to analyze and filter data, this is part of our evolutionary process. Humans now see more meaning to each personal connection, or interaction, due to the insurmountable amount of time spent on a smartphone screen, watching television, typing on the computer, flipping through social media posts, and clicking through video ads. Since we are all glued to video screens for significant portions of the day, our human interactions are ultra-sensitive as they are true interaction, not simulated on a screen, thus allowing humans an expanded interpretive ability of their surroundings and all actions within their surroundings. The appreciation for human connection will become more abundant in the near future with the saturation of technology and its manipulative condescending behavior. Humor is perception, it is freedom to choose a genre, or genres, of concepts, situations, statements, or physical matter that an individual interprets to be humorous subsequently laughing at, or "making fun of," whatever it is they believe to be funny. Humor, joking, laughing, are all used to comprehend our dream world where anything is possible, enjoying the unknown illusion of existence as we float in the cosmos. I personally use humility, humor, and comedic relief as a spiritual expansion technique often doing silly things to humble myself knowing I am infinitely tiny in the grand perspective of our entire universe, or God's penis as I am sure he would prefer. I am unequivocally ecstatic knowing that penis and fart jokes are fabulously fluent in the year of our Lord, 2024. As a sensitive man myself, I see an overwhelming number of radical rebuttals to overexaggerated societal quandaries that have no concluding resolution, only constant evolution, and I am a firm believer in reformation of the human mind. It is hatred that ruins the world; unfortunately, humor may not save it. The problem is our comprehension of another's genre of humor and our possible misinterpretation of the filtered data that we analyze. Our freedom to joke about anything consequently forms molecular hatred snowballing into an ice monster of cold, bitter resentment. A different perspective of our problem: We are all little bitches who cannot take a fucking joke, me included.

"Letter to the President"

Dear Mr. President,

I think you have an incredibly difficult job, possibly the most difficult in the world. I am sorry you are burdened with managing a country full of morons; however, I too feel moronic as I observe the world around me and the nonchalant corruption that powerful people flaunt with no remorse. Regardless of the general moronic population, we have many incredible assets and intelligent people in our country in leu of our unfortunate circumstances. The United States of America has more freedom than we have ever possessed prior, and yet so many people feel enslaved by our system, by our conglomerates, by our division of ideologies. How do you do it, Mr. President? How do you manage? In any given Presidential term, I know there must be millions of national inquiries to advise, to acknowledge, or to be present during credible moments. What are the issues that you, as a human being, are concerned about? The country's problems are obvious and ongoing; I want to know what you, the President of the United States of America, are passionate about. What makes your soul catch fire? What are your hobbies? What kind of movies and music do you like? What led you to become who you are today, and what freedoms do you hold dear to your own heart? Mr. President, I feel that our country has become weak by exercising our freedoms to berate you, your administration, and any United States Presidential administration. Although I do not wish to give up my freedom, or revoke anyone's ability to speak freely, I simply wish to voice my opinion about the butterfly effect it has on our country's wellbeing. Certainly, over the course of your life, in your career, you have committed shameful acts that you regret and attempt to block from your memory's cloud; I do not wish to discuss these acts,

I know you know what they are, and I do not wish to constantly remind you of the shame that is associated with whatever you regret. I have much respect for you, Mr. President, because I see the constant hate that our country breeds daily, criticizing you and our government, slandering your family's name, and examining your every move under a microscope. I cannot imagine the immense stress and anxiety endured as a U.S. politician or world leader. Mr. President, please advise the people of America how we can respect you more, and other U.S. politicians, knowing the corruption, lies, and scandal that plague our government daily. I cannot imagine the immediate pressure you endure, as a U.S. President, just waking up from a night's sleep. I can see the pain on your face, Mr. President, and I am empathetic to your circumstances. No U.S. President deserves to be hated in such crippling volumes. You are forced to make unbelievably complex decisions on a regular basis with certain consequences for either choice. Damned if you do, damned if you do not: The chorus of U.S. politics as you decide what you think is best for our country. I write this letter to inform you of my empathy and respect for you, the President of the United States of America. The media will paint as they wish their own persona of you and your administration. I do not watch the news for these reasons. I want to believe that there are good people managing our country, but the belief is simply a belief, an unproven reality. Our country's population is burdened with forming opinions based on others' opinions and the canvas they paint of our government. There are a number of political conversations that I am sure we would disagree on; however, you are my President and I thank you for your service. I am grateful to live in this Country and am honored to exercise such freedoms that many take for granted. I am neither Democrat nor Republican but registered as an Independent voter just last year. I am still skeptical about the worth of my single vote, or the majority votes of America; however, I am grateful for the people who fought for these freedoms that our country so arrogantly flaunts. I am unsure of the appropriate gratitude for such valiant efforts of warriors that have gone unacknowledged.

May this letter be a small step in the right direction toward gracefully thanking the good-hearted men and women who fought and died for our arrogant country we so proudly hail. A single Monday each year, dedicated to Veterans, surely does not fit the bill for commemorating human beings who gave their lives in a battle for the freedom we possess today; yet what do we do Mr. President? There is too much happening simultaneously to take credible time to fully appreciate much of anything anymore. I know there is an extraordinary number of people who go unacknowledged for their hard work, their research, their existence; let us give thanks to the unknown soldier and the battles fought unbeknownst to their civilian population. I would also like to thank any person that began their political journey by simply loving their country and wanting to help communities. I salute all who have bravely fought and who continue fighting. You all have my respect and will forever. Thank you, to you and your administration, for keeping our Country safe.

Sincerely,

Patience Zero, a humble American